# SOUTH

SOUTH AFRICAN STYLE IN DECOR
BY KAREN ROOS AND
ANNEMARIE MEINTJES
PHOTOGRAPHY: MASSIMO CECCONI

# SOUTH

south african style in décor

# south

## KAREN ROOS
## ANNEMARIE MEINTJES

text
LES AUPIAIS

photography
MASSIMO CECCONI

# CONTENT

INTRODUCTION 7

SKIN&BONE 8

SAFARI 48

KHAKI 96

CRAFT 134

ELEMENTS 186

DATABASE 188

ACKNOWLEDGEMENTS 191

INTRODUCTION

As recently as a hundred thousand years ago, the ancestors of all humankind were part of a single African tribe that spread out far and wide to colonise the world. And then some returned.

Southern Africa juts out to separate the Atlantic and Indian oceans, solidly in the path of Western seafarers, a land mass now covered by 14 countries. It has evolved a composite of cultures, languages and customs. The San and Khoi breathed life into the Stone Age; the Dutch, French, English and Portuguese settlers brought the styles and customs of their northern life, but were transformed as they met powerful black and Asian cultures. Nowhere is the interplay and integration of art, craft and culture as exciting as it is ... in *South*.

In this multi-ethnic, polyglot crucible, styles are fused, mutated and reborn. This book celebrates the clash and the compromise, the original and the evolved, the unusual and the conventional – with a twist. Paper-layered wire skulls revisit San drawings of the hunt and are a witty reference to the mounted-head trophies of stiff-upper-lip, pith-helmet colonial times. The pure, soft, whitewashed lines of the Cape Dutch farmstead inspire an urban minimalism: large-accent furniture, high ceilings and cool stone floors. Cloth intended to adorn a tribal dancer finds surprising new direction as a screen in a metropolitan loft. Boldly coloured Zulu beads that once denoted marital status or motherhood now run riot in chandeliers and figurines.

The safari gave us the game lodge, with its khaki, canvas and gin-and-tonic sundowners. Now the urban bungalow pays homage to the bush boudoir in diverse subtle ways: the open-air shower, the ochre-coloured screeds, the lapa and a lightweight, airy look for summer.

Industrial stainless-steel wire is crafted into toys on a sculptural scale. But do we not owe this vibrant indigenous form to the skill with which barefoot boys shaped the cars of their covetous dreams from baling wire and shoe-polish tins on lonely farms?

And the colours: the harsh sun adjusts the retina to a bolder palette – sheets of brash food-tin labels wallpapering a township shack use of colour and design to create home space. In Johannesburg, a 1950s aubergine chenille chair, sky-blue wall and lipstick-red pleated lampshades make you shudder, pause – and, yes, smile.

*South* is a journey into the interior and into the future, to the place we all came from and to which we are all going, in our own way.

SKIN&BONE

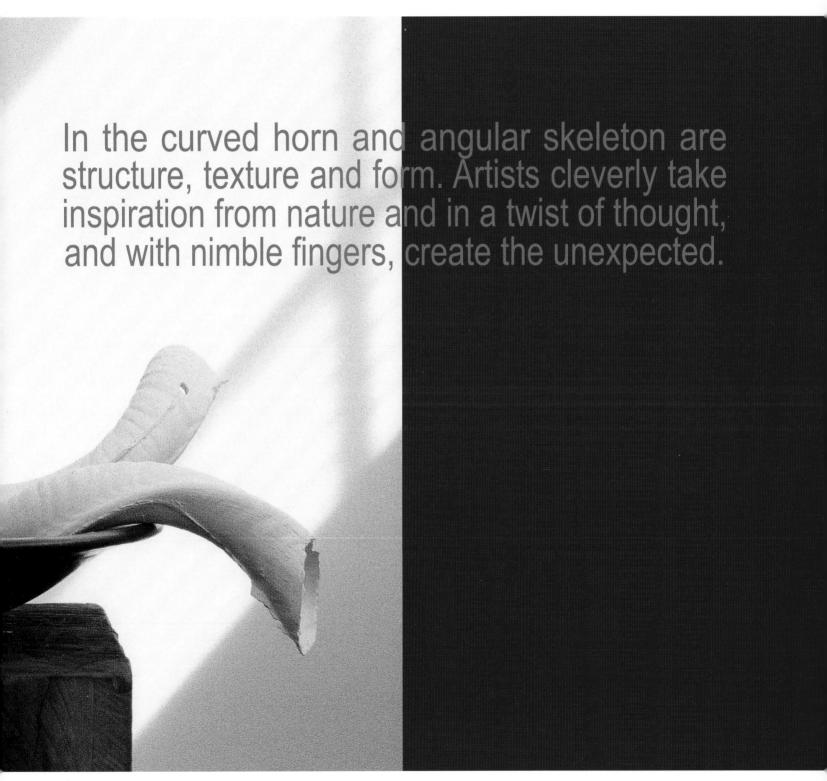

In the curved horn and angular skeleton are structure, texture and form. Artists cleverly take inspiration from nature and in a twist of thought, and with nimble fingers, create the unexpected.

Made from a mould of kudu horns, these unglazed ceramic sculptures transform traditional animal trophies into contemporary sculpture. A wooden cube of untreated timber serves as a plinth for both.

Anywhere else in the world but Africa, 'skin and bone' might speak of something diminished, of something that has lost its life and spirit. But here, rather than being what remains after the destruction of life, it is a distillation, a form reduced to stark simplicity. There are 'skin and bone' landscapes, poetry and images.

South African photographer David Goldblatt once captured, in a single black and white image, a desolate stretch of farmland in the Northern Cape bordered by a road. The near-desert Karoo earth was fenced with barbed-wire punctuated by split poles, bleached grey in the heat, that stretched away to matchstick height. It's a scene that resonates for anyone who knows the Karoo or Australian Outback. Earth skin, wooden bone.

In her book *African Elegance*, Ettagale Blauer includes a photograph of a !Kung San woman in Namibia's Kalahari desert. Slung shoulder to waist across her body is a skin kaross softened with ochre and fat and studded with metal beads and cowrie shells. There are other shells. The brass cartridges of spent rifle bullets are strung with leather thongs and clink faintly against the discarded hand grenade pins she has collected. The sound soothes the baby she carries snugly against her body. It is both shocking and insouciant. Mother's skin, man's metal bone.

On the thick reinforced mud walls of a 19th-century Cape farmhouse photographed in 1980, six matched horns serve as hooks for hats and bound clusters of herbs. Beneath them is a Cape riempie bench with its leather-plaited seats. Austere and functional, the bench is disarmed by three voluptuously stuffed springbok skin cushions. They are round to fit the awkward hollow of a human back. Comforting skin, practical bone.

Here and now in contemporary décor we find skin and bone, inspired by what has always been, but seen through fresh eyes. With transformation comes the courage to play. With wit and imagination comes transformation. On these pages, skin and bone on walls and floors play with their origins and suggest new ways to coax the eye into new insights.

The notion of a sporting trophy flies in new directions; kudu horns are no longer the booty of the day's hunt and a way of visually regurgitating the thrill of the chase, but become an artist's interpretation. They are no longer organic, horny growths from the skull of an antelope, but unglazed clay, fragile and pale, twisted into delicate shapes that insist you trace them with your fingers. They rest on a wooden block left to crack in the heat and rain, much like bleached bone in the sun.

Driftwood mimics the shape of trophy horns on a white wall. In another room, there's a visual pun on the stuffed trophy, combined with a playful sideswipe at the kitsch of ceramic flying ducks. Three wire heads dolefully look down on a reminder of their former life, a luxurious springbok-skin throw.

In a masterful play between original shape and man-made form, a vulture materialises in wire-covered paper and is lit up from within, a ghostly doppelgänger of a fierce scavenger.

Porcupine quills bristle from containers in almost every neo-Africa-inspired room and have become old hat, but, bound in the shape of an elongated Zulu shield, they have form once more. Wired tightly together, the sharp, waxy-textured spines are, again, dangerous at close quarters.

Architects and designers use some of these skin and bone images in their finished work, but often the feeling of skin and bone is just beneath the surface. Sometimes the visual clues are subtle.

To the far west of Johannesburg, an architect and client successfully complete a brief for a house that puts the natural environment first. Nothing should overwhelm landscape. Sliding doors open up to oversized frames for an exterior view. The chalk-coloured cement – crushed bone – of the walls provides contrast but doesn't jar. Weathered wooden decks and sandstone give 'skin' to the symmetrical frame.

In a photographer's home, rooms with cool turquoise-green walls are broken by frames and masks, paintings and real horn. There are chairs with zebra markings, both real hide and fabric interpretations of the black and white pattern. Skins warm the floors and back generously sized director's chairs. But the room is no old-style game lodge with the musty smell of cured leather – crisp white sofas, gilt-framed mirrors, kelim-covered ottomans, brushed steel and silver *objets* turn the tide. 'Skin and bone' is pared down to its essential structure and then given a new framework.

Nature serves as the inspiration for art in the camouflage pattern of porcupine quills collected on local farms.

OPPOSITE: Joined quills mimic the shape of a traditional Zulu shield. Cowhide, stainless steel 'Trial' chair and apiedoring wood bench set a scene of simplicity and restraint.

The vulture hunched over a kill or silhouetted against a lurid

orange sunset, often the sinister symbol of famine or drought

– and one of Africa's over-used, mass-produced images. But here,

in a pale, almost ghostly form, its skin translucent paper, its bone

galvanised steel wire, it is transformed into the benign. Stripped

of detail and far removed from its association with carrion,

this new creature makes only passing reference to its original

shape. For the rest, it is now a comforting night-light, paper

sculpture and a fine example of the way art can segue in Africa.

A paper vulture lamp and sun-shaped mirror are witty takes on a traditional African scene. Straw complements the light oak of a 1940s Belgian architect's table and Victorian fold-up picnic chair.

Africa guards Europe in this composition of cultural icons. A rough, untamed straw lion contrasts starkly with the smooth moulded plywood and chromed bent tubular steel base of Arne Jacobsen Series 7 chairs, circa 1955.

An upended linen basket woven from recycled plastic becomes a side kick for a black 'Panton' chair. A paper tube screen is a scene divider. Off stage is a zebra skin on an imbuia *maison chaise* and a side table in ebonised wood.

Skin for a hunter's vulnerable body, flesh for his belly, bones respectfully left to mark a kill:

this bedroom style plays on the ceremony and aftermath of the hunt. A black and white nude,

vulnerable and solitary, overlooks a low, flat bed on industrial wheels and wire footstool. Life is

stripped to essentials: a brown Nguni cowhide is both primitive and contemporary and a wire kudu

trophy with a paper skin looms over industrial 'bones', the stainless steel of the 'Diamond' chair.

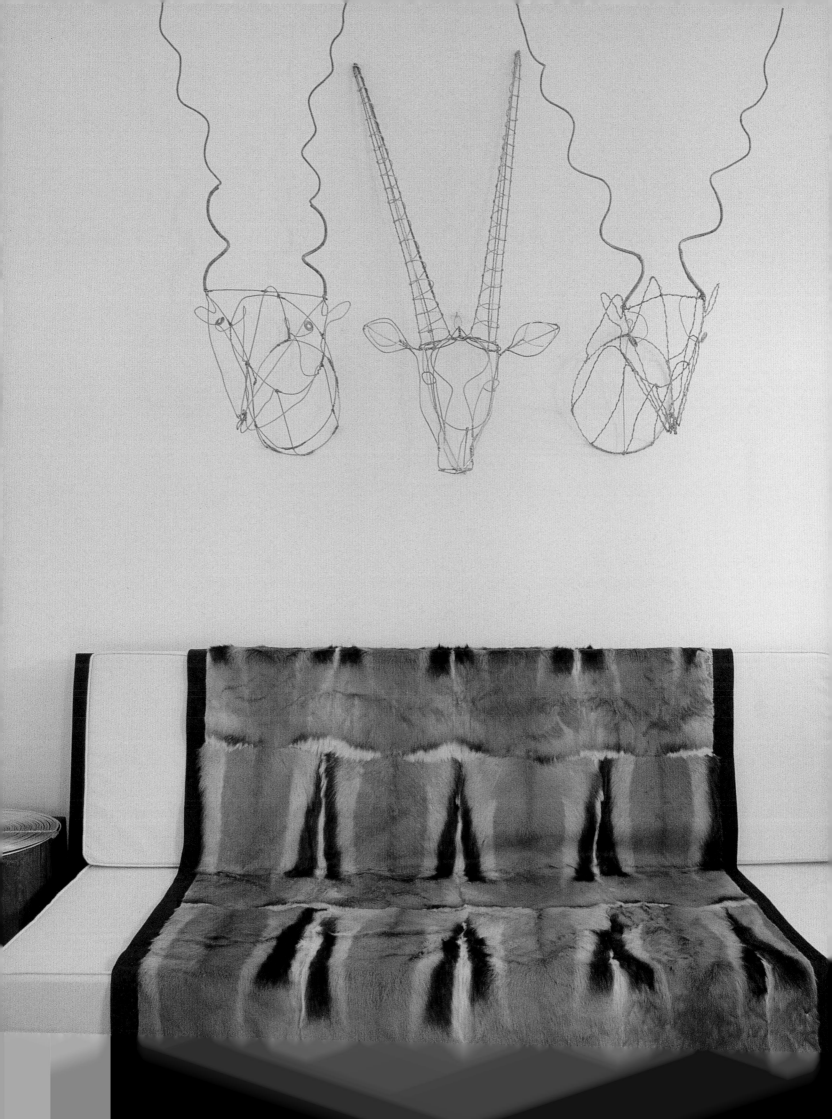

Kudu-horn legs support an antique mahogany table. The indigenous strelitzia flower is as much a South African icon as the 1950s Drum magazine print. The image overlooks a *faux* ostrich handbag from the same era.

OPPOSITE: Gemsbok, kudu and eland wire trophies hang above a springbok throw, creating an interesting trio of

African Crusoe: a canvas poster of a human figure standing on buffalo horns is the focal point of a room given balance by an untreated wooden cube and hand-coiled textured ceramic pots. A stainless steel 'Trial' chair provides seating for an art viewing.

RIGHT: Bought from a street vendor, this tough black refuse-bag plastic dog offers a cartoon silhouette on an improvised table with stylised ostrich legs. Block-mounted pages of an old art book duplicate the horizontal lines.

Nature's pin-ups. There's a witty interplay between photographed texture and reality as stone and nest overlook soft, white sheepskin covers on a slatted chair with decorative armrests

LEFT: Metal letters bought from a junk store are painted red to add eye-catching detail to a white wall. Set in a niche is a 'Rondine' Italian fold-up table.

ABOVE: Driftwood and fig twigs pun on traditional horn trophies and paper replaces crystals in an Ingo Maurer 'Zettel'z' chandelier. A driftwood chieftain chair calls the shots in the face of a cluster of translucent 'Mar' chairs.

About face. A hollow caricatured sculpture of a horse skids to a halt beneath the sketchy portrait by Kristo Coetzee. Adding solid form is an Art Deco couch in walnut and zebra skin.

# a RELAXED STYLE

The design concept of this Oranjezicht, Cape Town home combines private sanctuary and lively communal space. Key to the shared areas of the living room, dining area and kitchen (see following page) is a relaxed style. Furniture is generously proportioned and comfortable, inviting sprawl from family and friends. An out-stretched foot distance from a linen damask couch is an ottoman covered with a Persian carpet. A double fireplace in the centre of the living room demarcates the lounge from the dining area with its long table and simple jarrah wood benches. Windows cut generously into wall space allow in maximum light. Furniture in recycled wood, leather and hide provides texture and interesting detail in the main living areas where a purposefully stark neutral wall colour and a whitewashed wooden floor give cohesion to the style. Bedrooms are clustered and remain restrained, cocooned from the high traffic and activity of the central core.

A 1950s vase holds unusual blooms of kelp-shaped bark.

OPPOSITE: Two portraits taken by the photographer-owner flank a traditional oregon pine *koskas* (food cupboard) treated with silver hammerite and dove-grey paint. Surface areas are stained and varnished wood.

BRANCUSI

This living area is made continuous with the surroundings by solid wooden panels painted white that open outward. The white day bed

# THE ENDLESS HIGHVELD SKY

While the architecture and design of this estate in the Kromdraai Valley east of Johannesburg were paramount, sympathy with its location in the heart of the Cradle of Humankind World Heritage Site was critical. The farm comprises approximately 350 hectares within a 1000-hectare private reserve nurtured for decades by neighbouring landowners passionate about the environment.

But this was not always so for the 20-hectare site chosen for the homestead development. While it offered dramatic views over riverine forest to the undulating hills and imposing presence of the Zwartkop mountain, the site was characterised by wanton ecological destruction and an accumulation of debris. Before the foundation was laid, the site had to be landscaped and restored. The structures were designed not to dominate or impose themselves upon the land. They were to make the most of the vista of sweeping lawns, natural veld, water bodies and riverine forests, and the endless Highveld sky.

The sleeping pavilions are generously proportioned in their composition, each with its own discreetly private aspect, radiating from a centrepiece of indoor-outdoor lounges, dining areas and fireside nooks. The colours used are monochromatic. The minimalism encourages quiet harmony and an escape from the tensions of the day. The interiors offer what the owners describe as a 'blank canvas onto which we imprint our personal tastes'.

For the owners, 'Living here is a privilege. White stinkwood and bushwillow forests rise from the wetlands. Ancient African olives and acacias provide shade amidst vast areas of pristine veld. Everywhere aged rock formations rise from the earth as sentinels of bygone eras.'

The reserve is a sanctuary for human and animal integration with the environment. Kudu, waterbuck and bushbuck are common visitors, and on summer nights the call of the woodland kingfishers is everywhere. Ibis and egret rule the lawns, while recently three hippos adopted the many dams and waterways as their residence before being returned, reluctantly, to their home at a nearby commercial game park.

The owners' last words are of the harmony between the buildings and the land: 'If, in describing the estate, we have dwelt on the environment instead of the buildings, then that is a compliment to the structures and everyone involved, because that is the lasting impression and the aim of it all.'

The walls are finished with a chalk-coloured cement plaster that complements the floors of Spanish sandstone. Light is a prominent feature, and floods in through the four-metre-high sliding door that makes the interior and exterior one concept.

Ladders from Mali, chosen as a sculptural group for their bone-like shape and visual reference to the area's important fossil sites, are sentinels and silent witnesses to the kingfisher and passing hippo.

The large rim-flow pool lies at the end of a Balu wooden deck from Indonesia. The wood is not treated or varnished and left to weather naturally. The wooden African chair at the poolside is a Nigerian 'Stargazer'.

Benchmark design: an African fertility figure presides over a stark and restrained dining area separated from the kitchen by a sliding door. A stainless steel island provides a practical surface and hide-all for appliances.

OPPOSITE: Spanish sandstone floors offer a perfect foil to the mosaic of stacked firewood, treasure gathered from a fallen white stinkwood tree on the property.

Ebonised wood and custom-made Egyptian cotton offer clean and stark contrast. Geometric shape and the repetition of the square, masterfully includes a cinematic-sized view of the exterior.

SAFARI

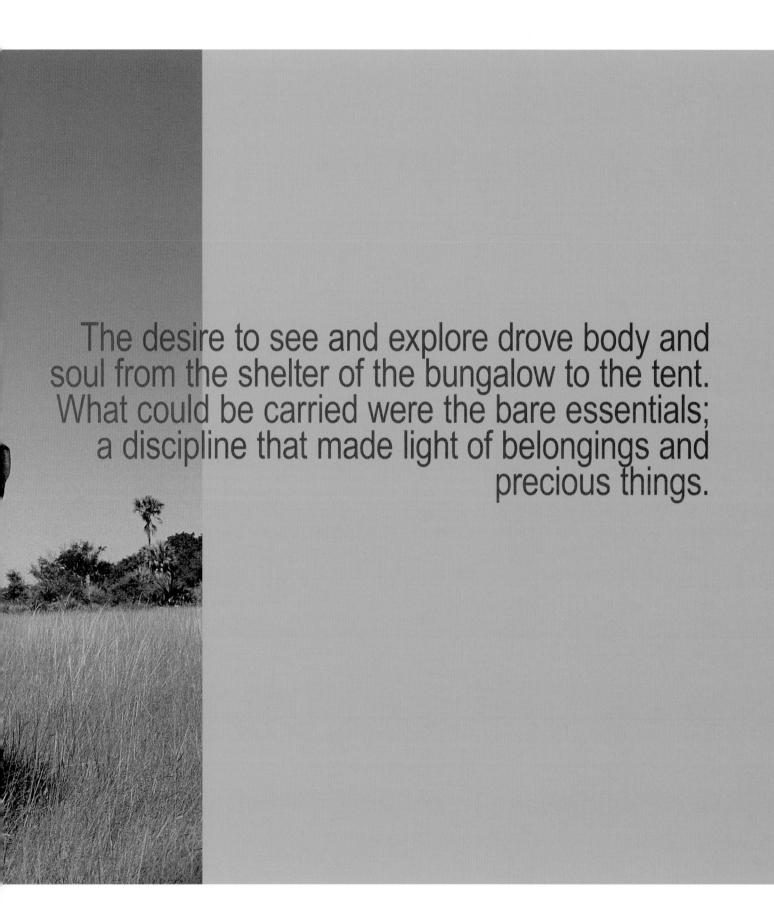

The desire to see and explore drove body and soul from the shelter of the bungalow to the tent. What could be carried were the bare essentials; a discipline that made light of belongings and precious things.

Maji Moto Tented Camp melds unobtrusively with the bush. Sleeping under canvas provided the original

safari accommodation in colonial times when local gun-bearers would carry an array of Western luxuries

to set up 'civilised' life in the bush. Today there is less silverware and ceremony but the romance and

lightweight, practical furniture remain.

The notion of the 'safari', a bush excursion to hunt and to explore unknown terrain, was born before intrepid Victorian travellers even set foot on African soil. The constraints of sea voyages limited luggage and furniture. Design and décor were driven by the practical considerations of this new life in the colonies – heat, dust, distance and a home that would be more canvas lean-to than castle.

The heavy, sombrely upholstered furniture of the day had no business in the new world. Light, sturdy wicker was portable and comfortable. Cane-backed loungers that allowed the passage of a breeze were cool against the skin. The folding steamer and canvas officer's chairs were soon *de rigueur* for bungalow verandas. The storm lantern and hurricane lamp took the place of elegant gas lamps and chandeliers, and the sturdy tin-lined trunk, impervious to voracious insects, took the place of the grand mahogany wardrobe. Set out on a butler's tray, with its simple crossed folding legs, would be crystal decanters and perhaps a silver hip flask to be filled in preparation for a chilly dawn hunt.

Although much pared down from the clutter and grandeur of Victorian life at home, safari style was hardly roughing it. The safari in Africa was adventure and sport with ground-level luxury, spartan by the standards of the well-heeled, but opulent in the bush context.

Perhaps in a corner, set in a brass holder, a potted palm would offer a splash of greenery, a sliver of a tree to represent the great forests of home. Elegant rugs would be scattered on the grass floors, silver and glassware gleaming in the lantern light and books for an evening read set out on small bookcases. Tents were up to a generous five square metres in size, one for sleeping and another for entertaining and work. Hanging from the canvas ceiling over the camp bed, a large white mosquito net would swathe the sleeper. Today, the look is considered the acme of romantic bush boudoir, but then it was simply a flimsy shield against the onslaught of insects at dusk and dawn. Water bottles encased in wicker were dampened to keep the contents chilled for as long as possible in the relentless heat.

Not all the finer elements of civilisation were lost. Elegant clocks were encased in sturdy leather with strap handles for easy carrying and as insurance against a rough portage over trackless bushveld. Today they are considered marvellously elegant and chic collector's items.

It is the luxuriously appointed tent and bungalow that appear now in a new guise, helped to fame by, of all things, the cinema. They may have evolved in Africa, but the 1985 film *Out of Africa* proved to be the hook that brought the world to the continent in nostalgic droves. Danish-born Baroness Karen Blixen, who came to live in Kenya in 1914 and wrote under the name Isak Dinesen, was the key character, and her wardrobe and coffee-plantation life spawned a passion for things African. The pith helmet or sola topi, the safari, lurid African sunsets, khaki and endless sky became the new icons of the continent.

Today, rustic game lodges and tented camps are the new-age castles. The folding canvas chairs and camp beds function more or less as they always did, and, from afar, tents look much like their 19th-century progenitors. But the safari is a more sophisticated game now.

Slatted wooden floorboards set out in interlocking lengths make for luxury terra firma. Persian carpets, dhurries and woven sisal rugs lie underfoot. Overhead fans powered by discreetly hidden generators are there for show, because air conditioning has entered the luxury hut. A shower may be set outdoors — a half-moon-shaped stone cocoon or cane shield under the stars, with a copper nozzle fixed overhead — but there the fantasy ends. Somewhere nearby, hidden by bush or rock face, will be a hot water geyser. Beds are dressed in crisp white Egyptian cotton and draped in mosquito nets. More than 150 years after the safari's birth, the practical still prevails.

Whereas safari style never found its way back to transform the stuffy parlours of 19th-century England, with their maroon velvet and mahogany, it has had a powerful influence elsewhere on contemporary homes and architecture. The bush camp has come to suburbia.

At its best, it appears with restraint, delicately extracting the best elements of the era and defining a new style: ochre-tinted cement screed floors mimic the compact and polished mud floors of traditional huts; replicas of Victorian ball-and-claw-foot baths have taken the place of the old safari tin tub; and wide verandas are shaded by deep reed-lined roofs, while antique steamer chairs and modern reproductions sit side by side facing the garden. Look for artfully arranged collections of silver and decanters or a paisley shawl thrown over the corner of a bed.

In the air, much as it always was, is the unmistakable aroma of dry-grass matting, wood and leather. Tented camps are not struck and moved, but have established roots. The adventure has come home — what has travelled is the style.

# MILLIONS

## of years ago...

Millions of years ago, subterranean north-to-south lava flow gave this bush camp the key geological feature that makes it unique. Singita Boulders, in the Sabi Sand Reserve on the western border of the Kruger National Park, uses the rocky hills – all that remain of that cataclysmic geological event – as inspiration for the rough, natural use of rock and traditional building materials. Overlooking the Sand River, the lodge camouflages itself on the site by drawing its colour palette from the dried putty-coloured earth, the weathered wood and grasses that are gold in the evening light. The underside of the silver-grey thatch is rich straw-gold; the soil in the shade, a soft ash grey. The concrete pathways between the tents is left raw to harmonise with it. The architecture and furnishings seem to grow from the soil rather than intrude on the landscape.

The thick base of desiccated palm fronds echoes the weave pattern of baskets and interlaced stone walls.

Dark polished floors, an ebony-wood sculpture and kudu-skin cushions are set against fresh white walls and contemporary shelf spaces. A central support structure of beams that reach to ceiling height is wound with grass rope to disguise the workings of the lighting system. The fireplace surround is a modest duplication of the exterior packed stone, and African print fabrics soften the lines of the built-in seating.

A refurbished Victorian ball-and-claw-foot bath rests on the slate-tiled floor and adds a touch of old-world living to this luxurious glassed-in bathroom. Blinds made from African river reeds provide privacy when unwinding after a game drive.

Hurricane lanterns and paraffin lamps on colonial safaris provided effective and economic light in almost all weather. They have become an enduring South African icon.

Stone, bone and rock offer natural contrasting textures and unusual forms, all an integral part of the sculptural features of Singita Boulders.

# A CORNER OF
# Namibia

In a grassland valley south of Damaraland, a remote and relatively unexplored corner of Namibia, rocks as high as two-storey buildings rear up from a yellow-white desert. For decades, travellers have come to see the remarkable San rock art of the area, but until Mowani Lodge was built, they had to return to the capital, Windhoek, without experiencing a night under millions of stars in an unpolluted sky.

The lodge is so cleverly built that from a modest height in a small airplane it is all but invisible. That's not by chance. It took the owner several five-hour trips north from the capital in a four-wheel-drive vehicle to decide on the site. It was envisaged that the lodge and camp would nestle on the rim of the ancient Doros crater but there were countless shifts of angle and position before this 'African village' – the words given to the architect as the design brief – finally took root.

The result is an extraordinary set of giant thatch domes that mimic the shape of the sandstone boulders. Set between the thatch boulders are 12 tents with wooden decks built to capture the camping, 'safari' feel of the lodge that gives visitors the sense that they are as close to Africa as they will ever be. The name Mowani means 'place of God'. For those who've travelled here, it is a place to stay in the wild that brings spiritual peace and rest for the body.

The name Mowani is from the Swahili word *mwane* meaning 'place of God' – and it is not hard to see why. Enormous boulders form nature's walls, providing a backdrop for evening entertainment: sunset, campfire and conversation. The natural setting is so striking that the cane chairs need only be simple and functional.

A marriage of geological form and architectural ingenuity results in

these domed thatch roofs, artful duplications of the giant boulders.

In colonial times, the veranda usually sported the steamer chair previously used on deck on steam ships. Its modern counterpart has kept to the principle of the cooler, the better. Cane and wicker chairs are set out under overhanging thatch open to the breeze. Gin and tonic is still the drink of choice in early evenings.

OPPOSITE: Canvas, khaki, wood and camouflage fabric screens merge Mowani Mountain Camp with its environment. In a certain light, the fabrics, stone and wood take on the slate grey of their surrounds.

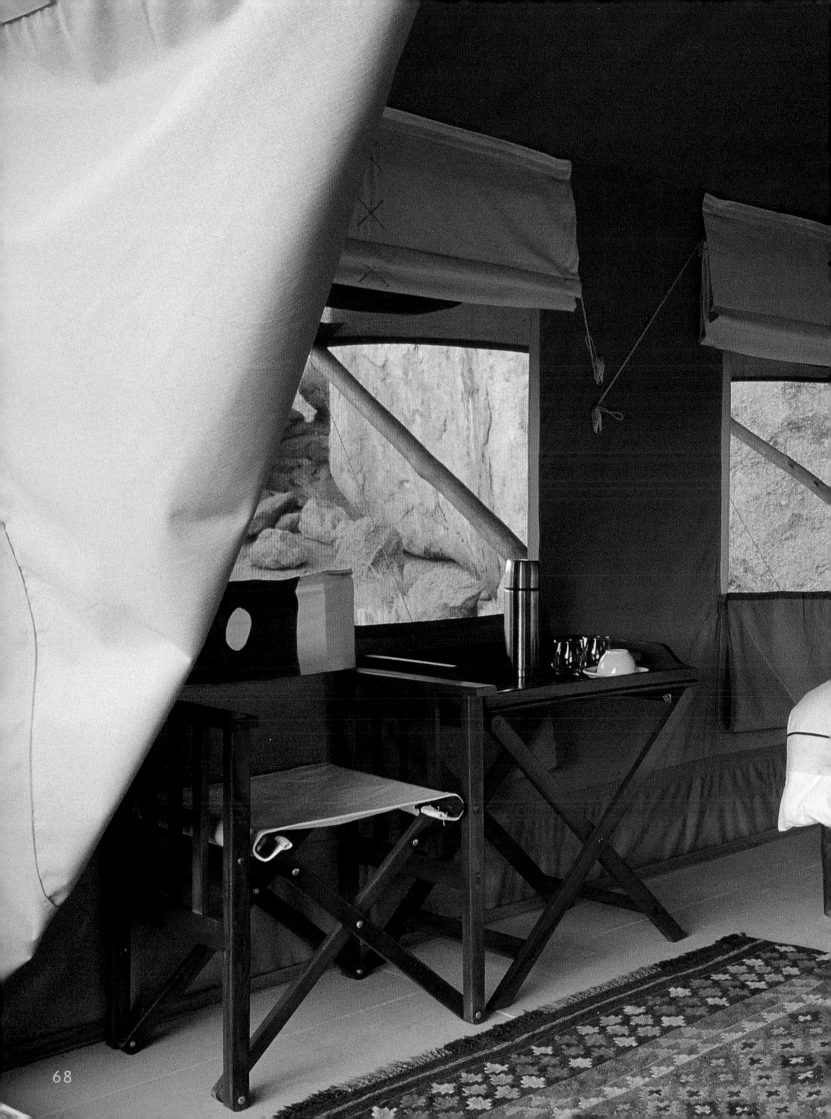

A simple wood-and-canvas folding chair provides seating inside the tent, while mesh panels allow impressive views of the surrounding landscape. Modern may mean minimal but bed linen is pure cotton and pillows are down-filled.

A simple line of sticks is used to create a natural boundary at Mowani and seems more of an artwork than a barrier, adding to rather than excluding the natural beauty of the landscape.

OPPOSITE An outdoor shower built of stone and cement is an exotic location in which to wash off the dust of a game drive in the warmth of the sun. The surrounding boulders give privacy and a tree

The unobtrusive, thatched architecture of the round-roofed huts is based on the architecture of an African village and merges with the surroundings to create a striking combination of line, texture and form. OPPOSITE: In the bush, conventional artworks give way to rock art, where the earth becomes both the medium and the surface of the work. Nomadic tribes made their artistic mark on surrounding rocks as mystical invocation for a successful hunt.

# touching the earth LIGHTLY

To meet their brief of 'touching the earth lightly', the designers of the new Kruger National Park concession, Singita Lebombo, responded with buildings that are part eagle's nest, part tree house. Perched on a sheer cliff top over the confluence of the Nwanetsi and Tsweni rivers, close to the Lebombo Mountain range in the remote, game-rich area of the eastern Kruger National Park on the Mozambique border, this camp is a tribute to light and air and the pleasure of the panoptic. Bleached wood, gum saplings, wicker, metal, floor-to-ceiling windows and wooden game-viewing decks complete the fusion of interior and exterior.

The design combines some traditional features – wooden decks, wicker and sapling roofs – with a contemporary sophistication to create a new African idiom.

The aesthetic of a minimal disturbance of the wilderness finds expression throughout: the saligna gum bath is stained to match the area's rocks, while the wool carpet mimics the colours of the grass in winter.

A hand-beaded curtain adds some flamboyance to the crisp cotton elegance of the main bed, while the wooden frame above the bed solves the tricky logistics of the draped mosquito net. The hanging light returns to the recurring nest or cocoon motif.

Each luxury loft suite opens to a game-viewing deck that is part tree house, part lounge, part communion with nature. Throughout the camp, the split-pole shading and woven branches filter, yet reveal, the shifting intensity of the sun.

The large veranda (next page) has views of the ancient mountain ridges of the Lebombo, the sustaining river and the savannah studded with euphorbia and aloes. Wood, wicker and cool white cushions mark a space of wilderness contemplation, the focal point for viewing, meeting and sharing the experiences of the day.

Perched like eagles' nests on a cliff top, these glass lofts bring a fragile touch of urbanity to the bush. They ironically reverse the usual convention of zoos and reserves. Here, the animals roam freely and guests, when not on a game-viewing drive, may be observed in their glass boxes.

The designers have chosen to combine Western sophistication with an African spirit, while

maintaining a strong focus on nature.

OPPOSITE: The combination of glass, metal, wicker and gum saplings blurs the boundaries between outside and inside, urban and wilderness, natural and man-made, giving Singita Lebombo a new edge in contemporary game-lodge luxury.

Open-plan living is favoured in the lofts, with floor-to-ceiling glass panes. The enamel bath is boxed with saligna gum and stained to match the area's rock, and the wool carpet mimics dry grass. Bush innovations include a decorative yet organic-looking glass-link chandelier.

The confluence of the Nwanetsi and Tsweni rivers is game-rich and there are

common sightings of the Big Five, antelope and fish eagles. The rivers roll past

Singita Lebombo's feet and provide a shifting tableau of theatre in the wild.

The bedroom is the stuff dreams are made of, with the main bed dressed in crisp cotton linen and adorned with a hand-beaded curtain. The hanging light resembles a cocoon or nest, a recurring theme in the décor and design. The squared-off mosquito nets give the sleeper more space and distance from the brushing fabric.

# OVERLOOKING THE CITY

There is something fecund about this African rondavel-inspired home in Johannesburg on Westcliff Ridge, overlooking the city zoo. The stand was originally jungle-like in its density and even now, beyond the wooden walkways, the foliage seems to threaten to reclaim its territory. And on a still night, the gravel roar of the lions carries clearly upwards and it is one house in the suburb where the sound is not at all strange.

The architects began building the house while working on Makalali Lodge, Mpumalanga, one of the lodges that has made them one of the most sought-after design teams in the genre. Like many traditional African homes, it grew organically around communal space, much more like the rounded pillars and chambers of a spectacular termite hill in the bush than the boxes and beams of an ordinary home. It is hard to see it as a single dwelling; it is more accurately a village interlinked with wooden decks and stone terraces.

In the central room with built-in seats, intense Highveld light rains in through a roof window and bounces off burnt-sienna walls. Then there are the textures: pigmented plaster walls have been left with their natural rough inclusions and where they join pillars there is nothing of the 'ironed crease' of a smooth-finish wall.

African images abound in sculptures, wooden carvings, masks and witty takes on everyday objects. For months, a team of African craftspeople using traditional skills made much of the furniture and gave the home its modern African space and architectural detail. There were no formal plans, only detailed sketches for the team to re-create.

The concept of a rustic outdoor bush shower with its classic nozzle gives one bathroom an air of a tented camp. The thatched roof is like a thick animal pelt through which trees, stripped to their bole, push upwards and outwards. Elsewhere it has weathered silver grey but is not cropped in a conventional strict line. Instead, it is left to fringe over the edges, like the coarse mane of a wildebeest. At roof height, a circular observation deck bears a striking similarity to the framework of a cylindrical Sotho-Tswana granary. It is no wonder that, when stepping through the gates of this home, one senses that the land on which Johannesburg grew was once much closer to raw bush than it is today.

While many settle for infrequent escapes to the bush, here the bush lodge moves into the city, with cool shadows, rough textures, natural materials and organic forms chosen for an urban Johannesburg home.

In keeping with the architectural form of the house, the swimming pool is spherical with a mosaic motif of a swimmer, by artist Clive van den Bergh, at its base. A sun bed from Bali, carved from a single piece of wood, is both art and resting point.

There is a feel of ancient Africa in the exterior design: the walled fortresses of Zimbabwe. The 'silo' on the roof is in fact a *sala* (African tree house) and an outdoor sleeping and entertainment area. There are also subtle elements from diverse cultures, such as the walled villages of Mali, clay birds from Indonesia and the African game lodges, that fit snugly into bush surrounds.

An oval mirror hangs above a simple stone washbowl with hollowed rocks tied to the frame as soap holders. The cylindrical metal roof lamp is a prototype of those at Ngorongoro Crater Lodge, Tanzania. Merbau sliding doors carry sculpted inlay done on site by carvers from Zanzibar.

OPPOSITE: Extensive use of wood, pigmented plaster and polished cement re-create a sense of raw Africa. Dominating the bathroom is a generous custom-built sunken Rhinolite bath for two and the shower nozzle is suspended from the reed ceiling.

Bold symbolic designs are appliquéd or embroidered onto the ceremonial dancing skirts of the Kuba kingdom in the Democratic Republic of the Congo. The designs closely resemble South African rock art drawings of the indigenous San people.

A modern white coffee table designed by the architect forms the centrepiece of a dressing room where elliptical shapes give an organic feel to the room. A semi-circular stone couch with simple white canvas cushions reflects the dramatic lighting and contrasts with earth-coloured walls and floor.

What began as the dun yellow-brown of a

military uniform became a notion of colonial

style; less colour than concept, less about war

and more about the embodiment of an era.

KHAKI

Cast in the vaguely camouflaging colour khaki, the colonial pith helmet protected settlers from the fierce African sun and was hard enough to withstand snakebites from above. In time, khaki also came to mean 'British soldier' to the Afrikaners who fought them in the second Anglo-Boer War of 1899-1902.

Could any other non-Anglo-Saxon word so short and so strange on an English tongue evoke so much? Its harsh glottal root is Persian and means 'dust'. How unpromising a start for something that was to have a life beyond a dun-coloured cloud kicked up by hooves! The British military captured it in the middle of the 19th century, first to describe the dull yellow-brown of a uniform and then as a name for the fabric itself. From dust to hue, from hue to the tactile, it was the camouflage of battlefield and bush designed to obscure man from man and man from animal. When the Anglo-Boer War broke out in 1899, khaki, for Afrikaner boers anyway, came to mean 'Brit' – and the enemy.

But it wasn't long before both colour and fabric shook off their off-colour overtones and became something quite different, synonymous with adventure, exploration and the hunt. Fashion finally put paid to khaki's dull reputation.

As Great Britain's empire spread, so did generations of colonial men and women, bringing with them a pared-down version of their lives at home adapting gradually to hotter climates and less formal social structures. It suggested a new lifestyle that simply didn't accommodate Victorian clutter.

Khaki jackets with military-style pockets and flaps were used on safari; beds were draped in fine mosquito netting; and furniture in bungalows and on verandas was more likely to be wicker, bamboo or teak. Linen, always slightly creased and limp in the heat, as if it had given up on starch and formality. Amid the rituals of colonial life – sundowners with ice clinking in long crystal glasses, church on Sunday and the niceties of a soirée – Africa simply demanded new disciplines.

Sturdy travelling trunks were lined with tin to resist the ravages of insects. Canvas buckets, compact camp chairs and hurricane lamps had to travel well. What came by ship was rationed by weight. The steamer chair, with its wooden frame, high back and light inset of woven cane, found its way to breezy verandas. Thrown over wood and tile, woven rugs were practical and were up to the beating that was their fate in Africa.

But khaki was always the common denominator. The dust was a reminder of its roots, and so was the wicker of outdoor furniture, the raw wood of newly built bungalows, kaross skins and mats damped down in the heat. The smell of khaki was that of raw fibre, cotton against skin, almost as potent as the smell of the earth after rain. Khaki was as ubiquitous as the high-pitched song of the cicadas.

Contemporary colonial style may veer towards luxury, with no regard for the constraints of trunk space, but still it is characterised by the broad, uncluttered stoep with folding chairs, crystal decanters and silverware. On the walls hang animal heads and a battered Union Jack, and on the wooden trestle tables are cloths of crisp white linen and perhaps an artfully placed sola topi or pith helmet. Below the ceiling, fans turn with a lazy womp-womp as they churn sluggish air. The thick and sturdy khaki of the military uniform may have propelled the word into common use but it's not where khaki's influence remained – or ended. Here in *South*, it is about a style and a genre.

A *bateau lit* mahogany bed with crisp khaki linen, late-Victorian pith helmets and collection of old rugby and bowling balls

These solid elephant bookends
from Mombasa are intricately
hand-carved from ebony. A 'Flos'
horn-shaped stainless steel lamp
provides background lighting for
late evening reading.

OPPOSITE: A horizontal row of
square-framed postcards pays tribute
to eminent Victorians and establishes
a theme of simple lines in the
bedroom, repeated in the design of
the mahogany bed, the blazer-striped
grosgrain of the bed roll and in the
zebra-hide carpet.

The image of ceiling fans gently stirring up languid, tropical air over a mosquito net-draped bed, or creating a small draft in a shutter-darkened room in Africa, is more about style than practicality. The fan evolved and came down from its impractical height. Table versions were more effective with the Bakelite desk fan (right) a personal defence against the humid colonies, as indispensable against the heat as gin and tonic. The brittle Bakelite fans became big in the 1950s with retro versions in red, such as this cheeky one, an instant hit.

The gentleman's club concept is extended in a grand colonial-style bathroom (next page). The antique copper plumbing and marble washstand evoke the institutional architecture of the public school and club, with a propaganda collage of Queen Victoria and the trades supporting the Empire above a set of shallow drawers from a turn of the century chemist. An Edwardian mahogany pedestal is used for shaving, and tiles are 18th-century sandstone and marble. A giant Union Jack hangs above a conventional enamelled steel bath that has been wrapped in sheets of copper plate, on a blackened cement pedestal. In the foreground is a teak plantation chair in which the arch colonist and erstwhile Cape Prime Minister Cecil John Rhodes used to sit.

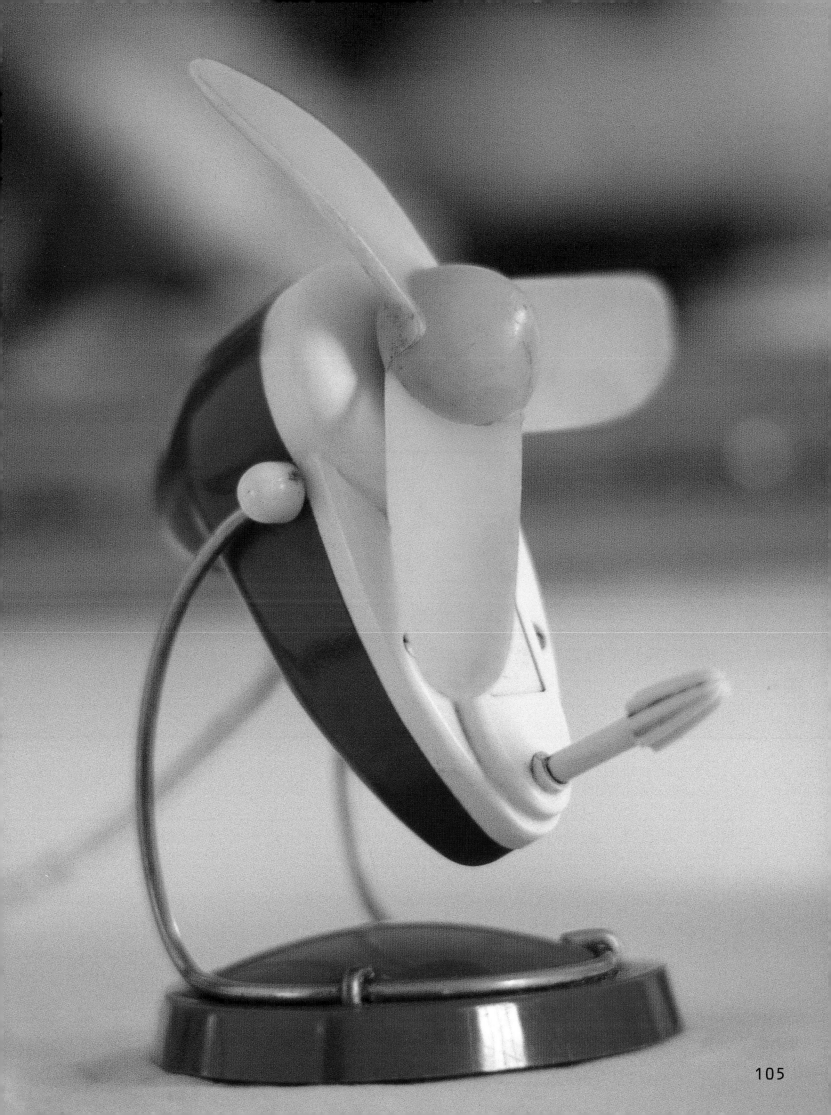

Traditionally clustered on indoor sideboards, elegant decanters and exquisite Victorian cut crystal are given fresh context in a bright outdoor lunch hour.

OPPOSITE: Hunting influences décor and dining on this stylish stoep (veranda), where silver trophies are reinterpreted as wine coolers. Folding Victorian picnic furniture in oak and a teak plantation chair invite a post-prandial forty winks.

Generous white shuttered doors open onto the waxed green cement stoep, where springbok horns, the head of a kudu and Victorian shotgun case that serves as a side table acknowledge a lifestyle of hunting.

The poet William Plomer captured some of the mysterious attraction of the veranda in 'A Transvaal Morning':

*And sharper than a quince,*

*Two bird-notes penetrated there*

*Piercing the cloistral deep verandah twice.*

Those broad shady sanctuaries became a distinctive feature of colonial architecture in warm climates. The colonnaded porch would funnel the breeze and offer a cool haven from an unforgiving sun. Often furnished with rattan or cane tables and chairs, they became comfortable 'rooms'. Part extension of gentleman's club with its table of silverware, linen, cut-crystal tumblers, hunting trophies, gun cabinets and flags, and part small drawing room open to the garden, one sensed a vaguely masculine, slightly faded elegance to the space.

A dramatically proportioned block-mounted protea print becomes an opulent headboard in this contemporary take on a Victorian bedroom. Bedside tables with stylised ostrich legs perch on either side of the box bed with wheels and, grand-standing in the far corner, a table with tribal feet is reflected in a mahogany *cheval* mirror.

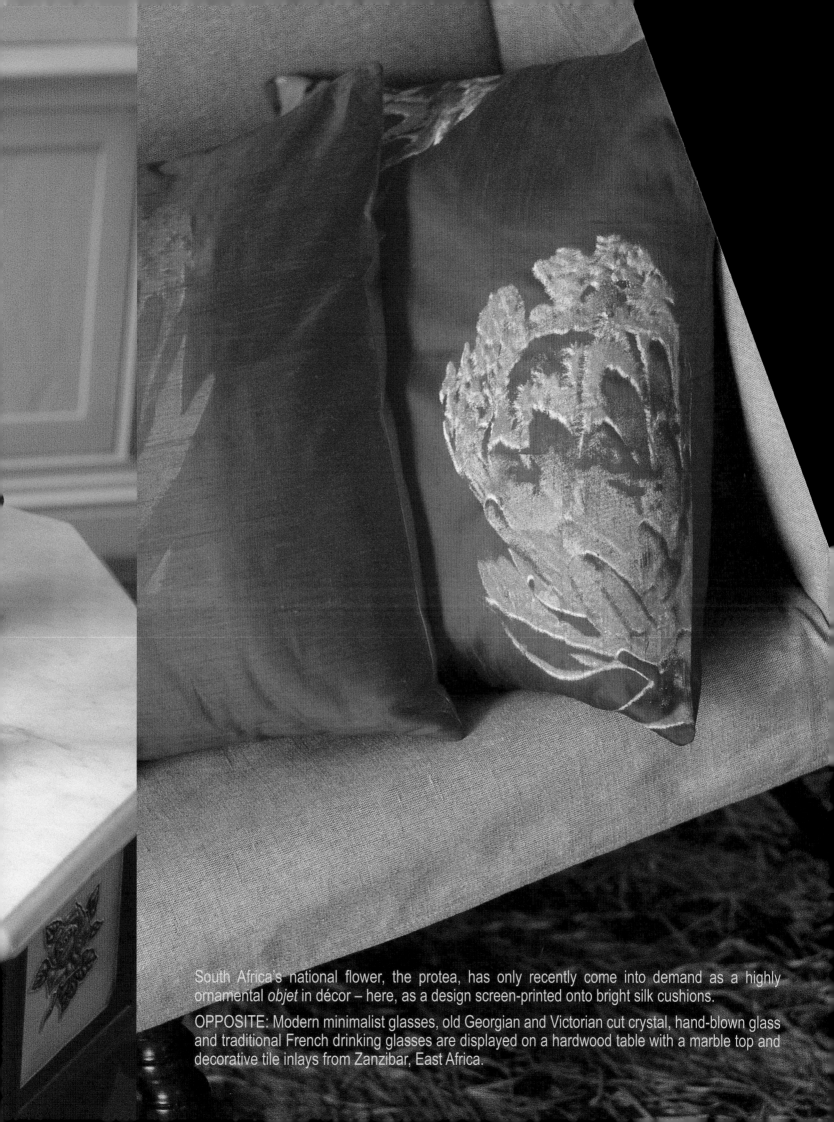

South Africa's national flower, the protea, has only recently come into demand as a highly ornamental *objet* in décor – here, as a design screen-printed onto bright silk cushions.

OPPOSITE: Modern minimalist glasses, old Georgian and Victorian cut crystal, hand-blown glass and traditional French drinking glasses are displayed on a hardwood table with a marble top and decorative tile inlays from Zanzibar, East Africa.

The painted table has a scrubbed pine top that gives it an understated beauty and a slightly weathered look.

NEXT PAGE: A delicate muslin canopy shades a long table and Victorian, French and traditional folding garden chairs. A 1920s urn from the old Johannesburg railway station restaurant profiles against a traditional whitewashed wall.

# SPACE and the UNEXPECTED

The Makgadikgadi saltpans stretch for hundreds of square kilometres, where once, thousands of years ago, there was one of the earth's largest superlakes. By night, it hunkers under a vast blackness shot with millions of stars. Those who've slept out here say the shooting stars are like celestial fireworks. Jack's Camp is here. And if the rains haven't come, there is not much else but the ilala palms that seem to spring incongruously from the flat earth.

Why might you journey to this tented camp in the Botswana wilderness? There are no luxury four-wheel-drive vehicles, only light quad bikes for exploration. Why safari in an area where there are no Big Five to notch up?

What this concession in Botswana offers are the ultimate luxuries: space and the unexpected. When the rains do come, and fill the salt pans, minute shrimp eggs, dormant in the dry pan, hatch and out of what appears to be nowhere, thousands upon thousands of flamingos descend to feed, a great salmon-pink cloud of beating wings. Then the wildebeest come, followed by the zebra, and predators in their wake. And then they are gone.

The deepest tone of the underside of a flamingo wing inspired the colour of the Indian cotton that lines the inside of the tents. They hold such extraordinary collections that Africa's skin and bone, the roots of khaki and the true and original meaning of safari – to journey – are drawn together. Forays into the land yield fossils and skulls that are brought back and added to clusters found by other temporary 'archaeologists' who have resisted removing anything from the area.

The tent is no spartan canvas shell with camp bed and storm lantern. Almost in defiance of the vast stretches of flat pan, here are rich polished wood, copper, brass and Persian carpets that create a cocoon of familiar yet unexpected things. References are colonial and, everywhere in these canvas shelters against a big sky, the broadest interpretation of 'khaki' is played out.

There is no electricity. At night, storm lanterns or torches light the way. When the moon rises, light reflects off the pan and it is bright enough to read by, strong enough for colours to be seen. Sometimes, camp beds are set up for a night under the stars: there are down-filled bedrolls, heated water bottles and, to break your sleep, the sunrise at your feet.

On the last page of Antoine de Saint-Exupéry's *Le Petit Prince* in his drawings of an empty desert with a single star, the most beautiful landscape in the world and yet the most sad, he writes: '*Regardez attentivement ce paysage afin d'être surs de le reconnaitre, si vous voyagez un jour en Afrique, dans le désert.*' It is here that he sees the little prince for the last time. But if you happen upon this desert place in Africa, he urges under the star he has drawn, don't press on. He may return.

There are baobabs, too, not too far away from Jack's Camp and the 'great secret' hidden to most adults (as told by the fox to the little prince) might at last make sense: 'It is only with the heart that you see rightly; what is essential is invisible to the eye.'

**5** Bedrooms have an air of East African style. Old Persian carpets are turned into opulent cushions that contrast with crisp white linen set out on a four-poster bed from India. Campaign furniture and collections give each of the eight tents individual style. At night duck-down comforters keep in the warmth of hot-water bottles covered in striped ticking.

Bathing here is an art, a ritual.

Interiors of the tents are lined with Indian cotton the colour of the deepest salmon pink of a flamingo's wing. The collection of books for guest referral ranges from Joy Adamson's *Born Free* to tales of the great white hunters of Africa. Framed prints come from Deyrolle on Rue de Bac in Paris, famous for its collection of bones and specimens. Campaign furniture – some original, some reproduced – honour a lifestyle that urged travellers to pack, move and explore further.

OPPOSITE: Fossils collected by travellers on desert excursions remain at Jack's Camp.

The arrangement of canvas-backed chairs, set out on an enormous dhurrie, encourages cordial conversation. Desert succulents are the 'flowers' for the table and pictures on the walls are suspended from fine chains attached to the framework of the tent. There is no electricity and all cooking is done on the fire.

From the khaki canvas of Jack's Camp, a metal day bed looks onto the vast expanse of the Makgadikgadi saltpans. At night camp beds are set up for guests under an indigo sky streaked with shooting stars.

The art collector-dealer who owns this home describes it as a 'black 1970s monster'. It was originally built in the old part of Blouberg in Table Bay, Cape Town by his parents. For almost 30 years, the house remained a tribute to the face brick suburban style of the time until it was gutted and reconstructed to include broad verandas open to the sea breeze, minimalist courtyards and colours as far from red brick as possible. The renovation is a work in progress with its spaces and lines subtely changing as the years pass. The house is a library of memories that reflects his moods and is 'impossibly sentimental', as it tells the story of his life. He retained the first landscape painting he bought with his pocket money when he was eight years old and a hand-written letter quoting a Breyten Breytenbach poem sent by a friend during his army conscription days. Older pieces from auctioneers' showrooms are in evidence, as he believes there is an identity and story to every one of them.

# a library of MEMORIES

The lounge contains an eclectic mix of ethnic *objets*, from the corner post of an African hut above the fireplace to local paintings made into a corner screen. An imposing sculpted leopard lies beside a cowhide carpet, matching the hide on the old Post Office chair.

An African sculpture, originally part of the base of an African chief's chair, looks from the vast bookshelves towards the table with its Turkish kelim, Moroccan fruit bowl and wooden dish from Alsace. The corner post of a traditional hut (right) forms the symmetrical centrepiece above the fireplace.

132.

Organic colours and shapes of a 1950 Portway picture blend in with the natural designs of two African vases. The roughly textured bowl in a butter cream colour is of a type traditionally used to wash the wedding loincloth of an African bride.

CRAFT

Here's the handwork of the mind's eye. It travels like language across borders, finding new vocabulary in wire, wood, plastic and clay

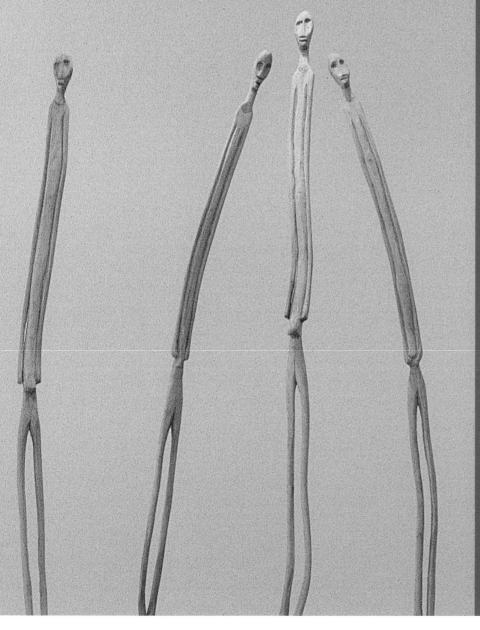

Bought from a roadside store in Zimbabwe, these carved stick figures, used en masse, reinterpret traditional African art in a way that suits modern minimalist and ethnic interiors.

'Craft' is working art that has its inspiration in a simple function. In clever hands, decoration and design make craft fly as an idea.

Colourful miniature masks are the identifying signatures of a tribe, three-dimensional passports that may end up as a traveller's trophies, transformed into a gallery of exotic faces. Wire is stripped and tightly woven with glass beads into swirls of colour and pattern to make bowls that cluster on a European coffee table. Discarded cans bearing First World and South African brands (Coca-Cola, Fanta, Castle Lager) are chopped, bent and sliced into children's toys on wheels that beat an uneven tattoo on dusty village roads. Toy then becomes naive *objet d'art* on a traveller's desk. The burnt-orange straw of a traditional Zulu *isitzolo* hat signifies the status of a woman; married, single, with child, of an age. Three hats equidistantly placed on a wall become fireballs of colour, a trio of lurid African suns collected as a reminder of times spent in a warmer climate.

Craft is born to be practical and decorative, and matures into the collectable. What seduces the eye of the discerning traveller is the skill behind the craft and its colour and form. When we buy a mask, a strange figurine, a voluptuous urn or a child's toy and relocate it, we give it a new and exotic context. There, in a loft apartment in New York or a semi in the heart of London or on a sun deck in Sydney, the displaced fragment of Africa draws the eye and arrests attention. That's the solitary beauty of craft.

But there is a bleaker side to what at first seems a fair exchange. Driven by a market eager to pay for little pieces of 'other', the craftsperson often learns to churn. And then what ends up in the corner of the apartment or on the hallway wall is far from a bold and original piece, or even an everyday piece that's flawed and striking – it's a cookie-cutter souvenir, craft with no soul.

On the stalls and sidewalks of prosperous southern African cities, souvenir and craft sit side by side, vying for attention. One is authentic, the other expedient. The objects have travelled with Africa's artistic diaspora and settled in the south, where trade is lively and survival easier.

But there is cause for celebration. To break away from souvenir art and feed the growing demand for original work, creative hands and eyes have begun to invent new art forms. The common wire daisy flower with cheap glass bead sits alongside a stainless steel brute of a wire Harley-Davidson, exquisite in detail and proportion. Wire is woven into a giant kudu head, an amusing parody of the mounted trophies that flaunt a hunter's kills. The ubiquitous African wildlife of photographs and oil paintings now reappear as paper-covered wire sculpture, a ghostly and luminous night-light. The carved wooden animal – lifelike buffalo, baboon or charging elephant – is pared down to skeletal form in wire and abstracted. Brightly coloured chickens made from recycled plastic delight us in a cluster, the trimmed plastic ruffles cheekily thrust out, like the petticoats of a Folies Bergère dancer, witty and defiant.

Baskets, once made in their thousands from reeds and raffia, are now woven with flat metal strips and stand an impressive three metres high. Left to rust naturally outdoors, their silver shine corrodes to burnt sienna. 'Craft' no longer means a 'little something' to fit in a traveller's moonbag along with a passport. To take this neo-African craft home requires planning and commitment. The result? Crafters design and create for a top-end market that rewards originality. The trade is a good one.

Even better, where once it was considered chic to stumble in the wake of international trends, smart southern African homes are now the first to use craft unself-consciously and to say something fresh. The talent that's left the north ends up south in homes that use Kenyan cloth, Zimbabwean wire, Zulu beadwork – and perhaps even a carved wooden coffin from Ghana in the shape of a chilli. South is simply where the clan has gathered, a Woodstock concert of handmade talent.

At night with still, long hours to fill, night watchmen on guard duty in the urban areas of Durban (KwaZulu-Natal) in the 1970s would patrol with no weapon other than a sturdy *knobkierie* (a wooden staff with a heavy carved end). Killing time by weaving scraps of wire around these traditional night sticks, the men became more and more adept at the designs. The craft of wirework was launched with modest means and scrap. Soon beer pot covers (*izimbenge*), traditionally woven from sorghum grass or palm, were refashioned from scratch with decorative wire and beading, and sold as fruit bowls. Simple functional homeware became art as the bowls often found their way to walls and were used massed for colour and texture.

Baskets made from grass and reed were literally given a modern twist when colourful telephone wire (the brightly coloured plastic-coated wire used in cables) was used to make a high tech and durable version. Demand outstripped often dubiously-sourced supply. The mainstreaming of the craft drove the demand for raw legitimate material. From colourful wire to copper and galvanised steel, bowls were no longer simply charming mementos. The 21st-century wire bowl is heavy with metal and as finely laced as medieval chain mail. Copper links catch the light and the glow brings a lustrous new texture to the design. There is no natural end to wire design and invention; a new kind of wire destined for the market has a fluorescent property and, by night, will create its own soft yet eerie luminescence. And from small bowls intricately woven from thin wire, craftspeople have taken courage and now create head-height baskets and vases made from industrialised metal packaging straps, galvanised or left to rust naturally.

WIRE

Traditional wire art becomes a sophisticated fusion of distinctly African raw material with a texture,

Galvanised wire art has moved from the realm of township art into stylish garden design and décor. Here, a miniature metallic windmill stands against a natural backdrop of pebbles and tropical plants.

OPPOSITE: This cool blue room is a witty melting pot of metals. There is a quirky relationship between an old-world fencing mask and retro Italian stainless-steel chaise, an ethnic wire rendition of a motorbike, and a homemade light fitting made from a bird feeder and wire mesh.

Africa is known for its original and innovative use of unlikely materials. Here, colourful plastic-coated telephone wire makes for an unusual take on the traditional hunting trophy.

OPPOSITE: This glass-topped table takes wire art from the realm of the curio shop to that of solid, functional, modern design. A wire elephant skeleton floats surreally above, an oddly weightless depiction of a natural heavyweight.

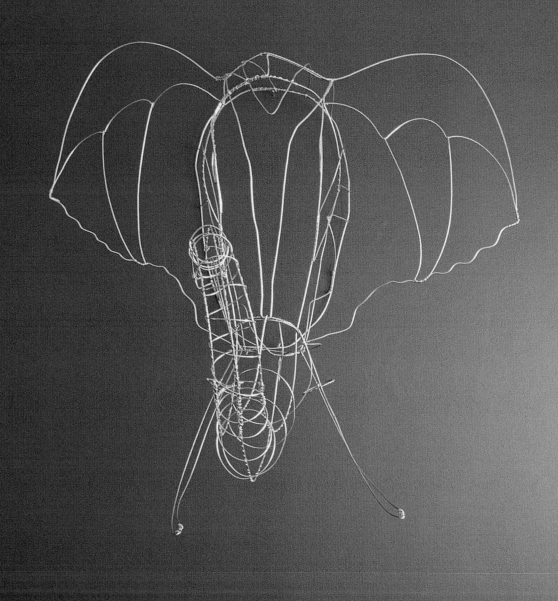

143

A lean, elegant dog stands guard at the entrance of designer David Strauss's home. The steel body, pebbles and charcoal-blue wall ironically reinterpret the suburban stereotype of Labrador, lawn and garden fence. The wiry hound also makes passing reference to the malnourished yet streetwise 'township' dog.

Weaving skills passed on from mother to daughter turned rough, raw material into an artwork that was not without individuality and design quirkiness. At first functional, what has emerged is a new genre of artwork so expertly done that it seems impossible that no machine was used in its making: a single 18-centimetre bowl can take up to 30 hours to complete. At first colours were earth bound and then as the reeds, palm and sisal proved to be the perfect matrix for exuberantly colourful dyes, a range of homeware emerged that rivalled any craft workshop in the world. Colour released an explosion of pattern – symbols, text and figures. And what began as a simple food bowl now appears in art galleries and sophisticated craft shops. Weaving includes beadwork as finely threaded as the silk of a Persian carpet. The beads, a legacy of 17th-century European traders, first used in curios, soon kept pace with a new demand for larger works, contemporary tones and designs that retain their integrity and yet sit comfortably in the most avant-garde setting. Buy one and tilt your face towards its base. If not long from its source, you can still smell the wood smokiness of the fibres as they are stored right in the heart of the home. Their origin remains the work of women, the skill still passed from hand to hand, but rather than a household chore, it is now a business where women remain close to their homes and families, generating wealth. It is an economic loop as critical as the continuous framework of the basket itself.

BASKETS

African reed and woven straw are the inspiration
for these outdoor, sculpture-sized baskets made
with metal packaging straps.

Carved from native woods, these grand vases are purely decorative artworks. With no distracting plants or dried twigs as contents, they embody African elegance and extravagance of proportion.

OPPOSITE: The decorative headdress worn by a *makoti*, or traditional Zulu bride (next page), also gives eye-catching colour, texture and form to a modern interior complemented by an orange 'Air' chair.

Made from densely and expertly woven coloured telephone wire, the spiral design of this basket is reminiscent of a coiled chameleon tail, or even snake. Outside an African context, the coil design is alluringly hypnotic.

Combining the indigenous crafts of beading and wirework, this delicate basket echoes the shape of a Barberton daisy, with a 'pollen-laden' core made from copper wire and glass bugle beads for the burnt-orange 'petals'.

OPPOSITE: Bold primary colours take this conservatory some distance from its traditional function of sun lounge for delicate plants. In their place are photographic prints of indigenous aloes in striking acetate screens above hand-woven plastic baskets.

The word on the street is this on the source of plastic animal art: in a society undisciplined about discarding plastic bags, freeway edges, informal settlements with poor municipal services and poorer suburbs are usually awash with raw material. Plastic shopping bags driven by wind like industrial tumbleweed flatten against barbed wire and concrete fences. Stubbornly undegradable, most of them might have remained pinned there for years but for the magpie eyes of craftspeople in the street who collected them to make wire-framed plastic toys, curios, bags and even lampshades. Again, buyers' demand for the craft drove a search for new sources of material.

New laws are limiting the circulation of plastic but factory shops that sell rolls of thicker, brightly-coloured plastic sheeting that feed industry now supply the ever-resourceful artist in search of material.

Central workshops have sprung up to consolidate production and vendors set up street-corner displays to catch the eye. Herds of black and white zebra, orange, yellow and blue elephants, multi-coloured ostriches and the original chickens co-exist on the pavement. Works range from mouse-size to a two-metre bird, smartly covering the tourist travelling light to the local with an eye for ethnic chic.

Paper art in the informal settlements also has its source in what is discarded, this time in sheets of factory overruns originally made for canned food labels. A flaw in the design also means the trash heap for the factory but material for the artist — and homemaker. The paper has a waxy sheen to it and finds its way onto the inside walls of shacks, partly for decoration and partly to paper over the fine cracks between the wood, insulating the interior against the wind.

Other paper and thin cardboard is sourced from discarded packaging. Products such as yellow and black Lion matchboxes, orange and black Boxer tobacco boxes and red and blue Lucky Star fish labels form découpage papier-mâché bowls. Andy Warhol's 'Campbell's Soup' pop art is art history and a continent away, but the striking repeat pattern is familiar yet fresh.

The faded paper packaging from an old
South African tobacco brand is recycled and transformed
into a nostalgic photo frame

PAPER&PLASTIC

Flocks of these colourful chickens, made from the plastic of discarded shopping bags, can be found on many South African street corners. This orange rooster struts in front of rolls of tinned-food labels, used here as graphic wallpaper.

OPPOSITE: Bright, branded wallpaper, made from slightly damaged overruns of canned-food labels, serves a two-fold function: colourful design and insulation. The patchwork quilt is a recycling masterpiece of discontinued fabric-sample books.

The wrapping on cans of fish is functional and fashionable décor. This papier-mâché bowl uses the overruns of branded pilchard labels to create funky art.

OPPOSITE: Painted letters bought at a hardware store spell out a pun on 'fanikalo', the name given to a combination of Nguni languages, English and Afrikaans developed decades ago by the mining companies to allow communication between a predominantly black workforce and the white bosses of South Africa's gold mines.

A cartoon-like plastic

zebra, made from

threaded and clipped

black and white plastic

bags, gives an amusing

slant on the traditional

hunting trophy.

OPPOSITE: Craft

becomes cheeky and

chic as a simple console

table is découpaged

with erotica cut from

magazines and flexible

plastic tube lights are

bent into a glowing heart.

# STYLE 'art house'

This is 'art house' style. On the Atlantic seaboard of Cape Town where light is strong and direct it streams into a face brick-walled interior where there is a fine gathering of works. The owner-artists travel the world and their collections 'converse'. Some of the connections are subtle: a William Kentridge drawing of two women at work, switchboard ladies wired to the world, is wall-mounted above a wire and bead horse, made by women at work on a beading project.

A brown leather couch by a British designer is set against a coffee table made from an old trek bed in stinkwood. On the table are old Zulu headrests. Now here's a dialogue between Brit, Boer and Zulu. With delicious irony, the former warring factions are overseen by a multi-media work depicting the first democratic South African elections. Of course, the art and craft collections intrigue and capture the eye and need nothing in the way of significant narrative. What's fascinating is that the collections fire up the imagination and trigger a personal take on what you see.

Textures range from soft kelim underfoot to Bakelite and steel. There is no colour theme; rather the colours form an intricate tapestry from wall to floor. For the owners, gathering the art and craft was for love and no grand significance, for pleasure not purpose. It's best that way.

Old Zulu milk pails make wooden vases that stand on a turn-of-the-century blue cupboard once used as a shop fitting. Above is a William Kentridge drawing, one of the owner's favourite artworks.

Stealing the spotlight on the sitting room wall is a multimedia piece by Willie Bester, depicting South Africa's first democratic elections. Below, an antique trek (camp) bed with Zulu headrests becomes a stylish stinkwood coffee table.

165

African design, form and colour predominate in a striking triangular beaded design containing a circular mirror. It hangs above hand-coiled ceramic pots and an intricately beaded African doll.

OPPOSITE: South meets West in this exotic exhibit of outlandish *objets*, where a medical cabinet from London and figurines from old arcade games are combined with an ethnic beaded buck and colourful Zulu dancing sticks.

It was the stories that their family told about this house in the Boland, Western Cape, that compelled the present owners to seek it out: fruit trees laden with ripe fruit, butter churned on the kitchen table, passionate Italian suitors, wood-fuelled copper geysers for bathing and a life filled with music. Family graves on the property tell of generations that lived full and productive lives. Owned by one of their grandparents, keeping the house in the family was an irresistible prospect.

The house began its life as a wine estate, but by the 1880s it had become a small farm and general dealer. It was thatched and sturdy, with four-metre-high ceilings and thick walls punctuated by large sash windows with recessed panelling and shutters. A veranda with pillars was added in 1900.

Later, when the present family owners moved in, the old barn became the artist-owner's studio. An enormous loft spans most of the main house and the storage room made of stone has remained, maintaining its usefully chilly temperature.

From a distance and in the context of its landscape, the house colours blend with its surroundings. In winter, its feet rest in a carpet of arum lilies and the 'Shiraz' coloured roof is in keeping with the winter vines. At sunset, with distant Table Mountain framed against a pink and blue sky, the house colours are dark stone and taupe.

Reconstructing the house was a physical and emotional investment and nurturing the surrounding land nourishing for the soul. The house has 'grounding' power, say the owners, and is somewhere to be oneself, to learn and savour the sense of history that pervades it. Most of the objects and artwork are made by hand, bringing their own energy and verve, a sense of history and their own 'battle scars'. It is a house of collections: the artworks and the spirits it has known.

# IN THE BOLAND

A cement baboon from Makasa 'walks' along the wall of the veranda towards a large wooden *kalao* sculpture of a bird, with metal decoration. It is the national symbol of the Senoufo people of Côte d'Ivoire and a good example of Afro-abstraction.

169

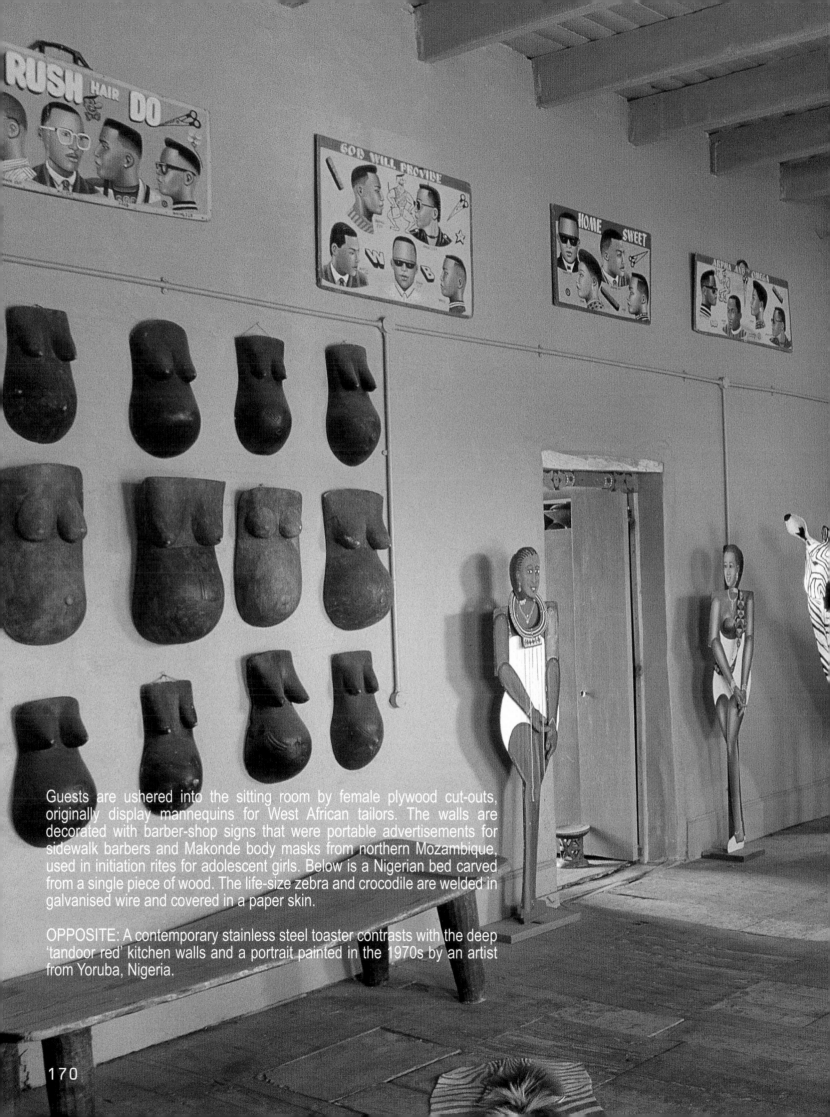

Guests are ushered into the sitting room by female plywood cut-outs, originally display mannequins for West African tailors. The walls are decorated with barber-shop signs that were portable advertisements for sidewalk barbers and Makonde body masks from northern Mozambique, used in initiation rites for adolescent girls. Below is a Nigerian bed carved from a single piece of wood. The life-size zebra and crocodile are welded in galvanised wire and covered in a paper skin.

OPPOSITE: A contemporary stainless steel toaster contrasts with the deep 'tandoor red' kitchen walls and a portrait painted in the 1970s by an artist from Yoruba, Nigeria.

Traditionally used as funerary totems, Madagascan *aloala* carvings have been made into an opulent headboard.

The bed linen is of Asante Kente woven silk from Ghana and the cushions are handmade from an old kimono.

The lounge is filled with eclectic African influences: a bright *tape* from Mali, West Africa, used by the Fulani people as a wedding decoration, becomes a striking tapestry above a round coffee table carved by the Bamileke of Cameroon. The large sculpture of a woman with a Zulu wedding headdress is from Ghana and the animal-trophy light is a paper sculpture by the owner.

Max the Weimaraner blends inconspicuously with the brown leather couch, camouflaged to hide himself from the illuminated paper animals that loom above.

This penthouse in Johannesburg is where craft meets post-modern. Religious – mainly Roman Catholic – icons are visual ties to the owner's convent schooling past. Colours are reminiscent of the interiors of African mission churches, but also of Havana, Cuba. Purple is here in accents, both as the colour of passion and of clerical robes. Works are salvaged from deconsecrated churches and sourced from a decorator friend's furniture and collectables shop. Pieces are chosen for the 'character-battering' they've received. Africa is not overt. It is simply there as a presence amid the voluptuous colour and velvet of rose heads.

# CRAFT meets POST-MODERN

Colours, textures and form play the leading roles in this scene, where plastic bags are recycled into a quirky flokati-like carpet that lies at the foot of a 1950s armchair in burgundy chenille.

Frames-in-waiting have been given a wall of honour opposite Indonesian puppets residing comfortably in Africa. On the table, a rack designed to store Zulu sleeping mats now holds rose-scented white candles.

Colour is courageously used in South Africa. In this apartment light coruscates off Indian Ocean blue and lipstick red. Texture is rich; lattice screen windows (opposite) make passing reference to Moroccan style while pleated lampshades, stretch net, *faux* fur and raw unpainted wood jostle warmly for attention.

Eurotrash chic goes African with a 1970s chair covered in grey suit flannel and draped with a Shangaan beaded cloth. A lounge suite in the Queen Anne style from the 1930s or 1940s squats overstuffed and unrepentantly scruffy. The view it offers is of display cabinets containing key items: a Sylvac dog and a Crown Devon Art Deco vase. Behind them, a rack for Zulu sleeping mats is reconstituted as a decorative skirting board.

# ELEMENTS

Africa has a way of making the most of its bare essentials and has developed a spirit of resourcefulness. Early settlers found that there was virtually no stone that could be easily quarried, locally made bricks weathered badly, timber suitable for building had to be imported and roofing tiles were not available. The land became the natural storehouse: sticks, grass, clay and stones – cheap, durable and attractive materials – were used for shelter, interiors and decoration. Thick coats of white limewash, textured weather-worn woodwork, dark, velvety thatch, bright Ndebele designs on clay walls – all are a celebration of Africa's basic elements. Whether in the system of building, the materials used for architecture or the ways in which walls are made beautiful, natural objects are used innovatively. Southern Africa has a history peppered with originality and creativity.

stone

For material so unyielding in tone and reputation, stone is fluid. It has been used since the earliest times for its strength, convenience, visual beauty and resistance to wind and corrosive climates. It forms foundation, wall and step. It is both the earliest artist's palette and the bare face for a decorator's hand. It is both destructive weapon and builder's fine 'lace'. Strung together in thin layers, it is precarious in part, yet formidable as a whole.

Stone works. In 19th-century gold-rush times, large boulders were used to crush quartz to extract precious ore.

Stone is monument. On finding the lush, hospitable shores of the Eastern Cape in 1487, explorer Bartholomeu Diaz erected a limestone cross two metres high to mark his discovery, 165 years before the first settlers arrived. Less ornate stone cairns mark death and direction.

Stone is artistic legacy. On cave walls and rocky outcrops, from Mpumalanga to the Western Cape, leaping figures and stylised creatures drawn by the indigenous San tell an epic story of dreams and the hunt. In the Eastern Cape, powdered stones mixed with oil made a sturdy paint.

For rural tribes from Lesotho to Mpumalanga stone is shelter. A circle of blocks laid on the ground and built on layer by layer, with the edges projecting inwards, form a small, impenetrable fortress. Adroitly built beehive huts offer shelter.

Walls of dry-packed stone form a strong barrier of intricately connected sandstone. Used before the invention of cement, the primitive method resurfaces in game lodges and African-style homes of today. The technique is remarkably unchanged. There is faith in a stone's weight and protective power, and there is beauty. Robben Island's quarried green-blue slate and soft white sandstone graces table top and wall. On the floors of Groot Constantia and the Castle of Good Hope, dark-red Steenberg stone, quarried for 19th-century imperialist and business magnate Cecil John Rhodes, still lies underfoot today.

Sandstone and shale, slate and granite: stone is cool and contemporary. Polished granite is now slick kitchen worktop and slate, neutral floor. Stone is 'clay' in an architect's hands.

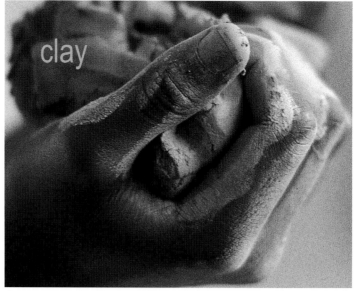

clay

Pottery, mosaics, porcelain, bricks ... clay is pay dirt for art and architecture. Mouldable and malleable, it's the background material of 10,000 years of man's recorded history. It was simply always there, at his feet. Clay is nature's plastic that stretches its form to accommodate.

Soon it carried water and was shaped into beads to be threaded on leather and twine. It was turned into overlapping, interlocking fireproof tiles, squared off and baked for brick, coiled and flattened in snake-like whirls for pots carried head-high from river to hut.

Clay bricks built the 18th-century Cape on the back of slaves. In droves they dug up and watered the soil, and ground it to a powdery pulp under the weight of horses. Thousands of hands kneaded the pulp into rough bricks that were shaped in moulds, sun-dried and baked in kilns. The walls grew strong on sweat.

In Xhosa villages in the Transkei, Ciskei and Eastern Cape, sun-dried mud bricks, or poles and clay, grew to wall height by family hands. Clay was used to make richly ornamented screens that served as partitions in early rectangular huts before walls were common dividers. Some remained unadorned while on others, symbolic designs were patterned by fingers, hands, rags or brushes, creating decoration and identity. The brightly painted geometric murals of Ndebele mud-brick homes north-east of Pretoria became African icons.

The walls of many early settler cottages were made from mud, unburnt brick and rubble bonded with clay, and the original floors of most Cape Dutch homes were solid clay, often embedded with peach stones. While these floors were rubbed weekly with animal blood to preserve them, in traditional rural huts the cheaper option of cow dung was used. Sweat, blood, pigment and dung – clay absorbs and yields to foot, hoof and hand.

wood

Under a microscope, wood cells are dicotyledonous fingerprints as unique as the whorls on a human fingertip. Wood provides the building blocks of the imagination and can be fashioned into anything from decorative beads, sculpture, ships and musical pipes to lurid masks for warding off evil spirits.

Practical, durable, renewable, natural, wood is sacred ecologically and spiritually – from totemic idols and the imagery of the tree of life to the cross of the Crucifixion.

In Africa, wood is shelter, fuel and a receptacle for water and food. Here, south of the equator, and long before the sturdy Cape Dutch architecture of the 17th, 18th and 19th centuries, the indigenous Khoikhoi made a beehive shelter with interlocking framework of saplings covered with animal skins or reed mats. Other indigenous peoples constructed similar wooden frames. Wood was a fragile barrier against the wild.

Later, varieties of wood grains, colours, angles and textures were used for panelling, cabinets and floors. Indigenous kamassi wood was used for veneering, olive wood – strong and brown-coloured, with a beautiful grain – for furniture, assegai for chairs, rooi els and wit els for carving, and wild chestnut and Cape beech for furniture and panelling, yellowwood – rich and earth-yellow in colour, with a beautiful grain – made floors, ceilings and inlay on tables. Stinkwood, a very durable and handsome timber varying in colour from light brown to black, was used for furniture and joinery, frames and doors.

But indigenous timber suitable for building was scarce.

The Dutch East India Company brought in ebony and teak from Indian Ocean islands. Later, trees shipped from Europe and Australia – pine and wattle in particular – took root and flourished, serving industry and a population hungry for building material. In the centuries to come, these aliens would threaten to overwhelm indigenous species.

Modern architects now let wood weather outside, allowing it to bleach grey under a harsh sun. Outdoor living has given rise to the sun deck, while the mark of a good game lodge is its wooden observation deck.

Today, informal settlements without foundations cluster on the outskirts of cities. Wood is gathered from industry that discards it. Doors, windows, frames, shutters and simple furniture are fashioned from old wooden packing cases and from any other wood that's survived its industrial life in factory and warehouse.

Alien trees gone wild in a fertile climate are cut for firewood and wound into works of art (giant cocoon-shaped pots and garden archways) and windbreaks set into sand dunes protect the fragile indigenous vegetation. Malleable wood endures and serves us well.

lime

straw and sapling

The tightly interwoven twigs and branches of early traditional dwellings resisted the point and thrust of both 'assegai and musket ball', say the early explorers who diarised their observations. They noted that 'not one smallest twig projected beyond the surface, which was even as that of a basket.' Above, thatch grass is layered thick and bound with acacia bark to make it resistant to wind and to repel rain. Atop stone walls, meticulous fences of twigs formed vertical patterns while thatched conical domes, as silky as an animal pelt, would offer contrasting texture and shape. As the thatch weathered, it would meld into the landscape, well camouflaged against rock and veld.

Defence and shelter, yes, but there is no rough and readiness about it. Simple, functional and beautiful, sapling and straw provide inspiration for contemporary architecture and a lesson in the restraint of 'touching the earth lightly'.

Roughly plastered walls coated with thick layers of white limewash are characteristic of the south, but a thousand years lie behind its use. Brick, stone, mud and timber-fram buildings all leant on lime as a vital ingredient in mortar, plaster and decoration long before cement appeared.

Calcareous remains of corals and shells on the sea bed formed the basis of lime used in the south, and the Cape coast was a rich source. Massive deposits of shell found on Robben Island led to a flurry of building, and no wonder: lime plasters and washes miraculously prevented damp, mould and condensation. Soft but tough, lime adapted like a living organism to seasonal and climatic changes in humidity and temperature.

Fishermen's cottages, with their annual coat of chalky whitewash over thick, mud-plastered outer walls, stood out starkly against a green coastline. In rural areas, 'dagha', a mixture of lime and fresh cow dung, sealed and smoothed surfaces. Lime was egalitarian, though. A well-matured lime putty diluted in water to make a cheap, durable skin was also used liberally by the European settlers on the walls of their Cape Dutch houses. Despite modern alternatives, the wet slaked-lime putty of old is still used. Its original properties hold fast.

# DATABASE

For full contact details, see Directory.

## 1. skin & bone

p.8-9
Ceramic kudu horns
By Anthony Harris and Gerhard Swart
Ceramic Matters
Colours: white or rust finish
Wooden block
Available from Egg Design

p.13
Wooden bench
By Edzard du Plessis
Available from MG Design Box
Stainless steel 'Trial' chair
From the Indecasa range
Available from European Concepts

p.15
Light
By Michael Methven

p.16-17
Straw lion
By Felix Chikanya
Available from artist
Arne Jacobsen Series 7 chairs
Sold under licence by Fritz Hansen

p.18-19
Day bed
Available from Generation Furniture
'Panga' Donghia side table
By OKHA Interiors
Also available in ducoed and pearlised finish
Prints
Photographer: Dook, from his book Skin and Bone

p.21
Cowhide bed cover
Available from Incanda: Décor Out of Africa
Kudu trophy
By Michael Methven
'Diamond' chairs
By Harry Bertoia for Knoll
Available from Limeline
Wire stool
By Warren Platner for Knoll
Available from Limeline
Portrait
Photographer: Jacqui Sinclair
From The Photographers Gallery ZA

p.22
Wire trophies
By Winston Rangwani
Available from Streetwires
Springbok kaross
Available from Baroness von den Mess
Donghia day bed
Available from OKHA Interiors

p.23
Antique table
From House Rules
Photograph from Drum magazine
Photographer: Jürgen Schadeberg

p.24-25
Ceramic pots
By Titus Steyn
Treatment: left roughly textured, stained black and polished to a sheen
Poster
Photographer: Dook, from his book Skin and Bone
Printed by The Scan Shop

Stainless steel 'Trial' chair
From the Indecasa range
Available from European Concepts
Wooden block
Available from Egg Design

p.25
Ceramic pots
By Barbara Jackson
Available from Heartworks

p.26-27
Multimedia artworks
By Stephen Inggs

p.28
Rondine Italian fold-up table
Supplier: Magis
Available from ID Solutions
Poster
Nicci, photographed by Dook, from his book, Skin and Bone

p.28-29
'Mar' chairs
Available from European Concepts
Chandelier
By Ingo Maurer
Chieftain chair
By Mano Kristallis
Wooden block
Available from Egg Design

p.30
Horse sculpture
By Keith Jordaan
Portrait
By Kristo Coetzee

p.35
Portraits
Photographer: Estelle Lampbrecht

p.36
Namgi fertility and protection dolls
From Cameroon
Sourced by Mark Valentine of Amatuli Fine Art
Architects
Louis Louw Johan Bergenthuin Architects

p.40
Mali ladders
Sourced by Mark Valentine of Amatuli Fine Art

p.43
'Stargazer' chair
Sourced by Mark Valentine of Amatuli Fine Art

p.44
Kitchen unit
By O + R Exclusive Creations
Photograph
Photographer: Merwelene van der Merwe
Fertility figurine
Sourced by Totem Gallery

## 2. safari

p.48-49
Location
Abu's Camp, Randall Moore Elephant Back Safaris
Photograph
Photographer: Dook

p.50-51
Location
Maji Moto Tented Camp, Conservation
Corporation Africa, Tanzania
Bush architect: Silvio Rech
Photograph
Photographer: Dook

p.55-61
Location
Singita Boulders and Singita Ebony

p.62-64
Photograph
Visi magazine

p.66
Interior
Décor advisor: Heidrun Diekman

p.67
Photograph
Visi magazine

p.68-69
Interior
Interior designer: Tanya Komen
Photograph
Visi magazine

p.70-73
Photograph
Visi magazine

p.75
Location
Singita Lebombo
Designer: Boyd Ferguson
Architects: Andrew Makin and Joy Brasler

p.76-77
White cushions and stools
By the LOSA (London-South Africa) project
Organic wicker chairs
By Roderick Vos

p.82
Interiors
By Boyd Ferguson
Table
By Boyd Ferguson
Glass-link chandelier
By Boyd Ferguson

p.84-85
Bedside lamp
By Julia Leakey
Beaded curtain
By Boyd Ferguson
Table
By Boyd Ferguson

p.93
Metal bathroom light
By Silvio Rech

p.94
Kuba ceremonial dancing skirt
Sourced by Kim Sacks Gallery

p.95
Coffee table
By Silvio Rech

## 3. khaki

p.100-101
Bateau lit bed (sleigh bed)
Available from Hans Van Der Merwe & Sons

p.102
Lamp
Available from European Concepts

p.103
Pictures
National Portrait Gallery, London

p.112-113
Vase in mirror
Available from Ceramic Matters

Bedside tables
Rondine Italian fold-up table
Supplier: Magis
Available from ID Solutions
Protea picture
Photographer: Lien Botha

p.114
Glasses
Available from Plush Bazaar

p.115
Protea pillows
By Design Team from Pretoria Technikon
Available from Loads of Living

p.118-119
Photograph
From *Outdoor Living*, by Karen Roos and Annemarie Meintjes

p.120-127
Photographs
Shot on location at Jack's Camp, Uncharted Africa
Safari Company
Photographer: Dook

p.128-129
Decorator
David Strauss of Strauss Interiors
Lily paintings
By Leon Vermeulen

p.130
Sculpture
From Totem Gallery
Photographer: Alain Proust for *Visi* magazine

p.132
African pots
From Totem Gallery
Portway paintings:
From Natalie Knight Gallery
Photograph
Photographer: Alain Proust for *Visi* magazine

## 4. craft

p.134-135
Wooden carved stick-men
From the collection of Jenni Button of Philosophy

p.139
Wire vases
Available from Streetwires

p.140
Windmills
Available from Streetwires
Photograph
Photographer: Paul Gordon

p.141
Wall paint
Colour: Plascon Blue Spruce
Motorbike
Available from Streetwires
Fencing mask
Available from Baroness von den Mess
Stainless-steel chaise
Original 1950s design by Harry Bertoia

p.142
Wire trophy
By Spear and Delingo

p.143
Elephant trophy and table
Available from Streetwires

p.144-145
Wire dog
From David Strauss' personal collection
By local street vendor

p.146
Basket on left
By Keanu Visser
Available from Montebello Design Centre (galvanised or rusted)

p.148
Large wooden vases
By Boyd Ferguson
Displayed in interior of Singita Lebombo Game Lodge

p.149
Zulu headdress
Available from Art Africa
'Air' chair
By Jasper Morrison
Supplier: Magis
Available from ID Solutions

p.150
Spiral basket
Available from Art Africa

p.152
Wire and bead bowl
Available from Art Africa

p.153
Baskets
Available from Heartworks
Aloe acetate screens:
Photographer: Lien Botha
Printed by The Scan Shop

p.155
Frame
Available from Pan African Market

p.156
Photograph
Photographer: Craig Fraser, from his book *Shack Chic*, published by Quivertree Publications, South Africa.
Canned-food labels
Available very cheaply from street vendors in informal settlements

p.158
Pilchard bowl
Available from Heartworks

p.159
Colourful paper labels
Available at many bus stops in the informal settlements
Plasticware
Available from local supermarkets

p.160
Zebra trophy
Supplied by Michael Methven

p.161
Table
Découpage by Sarah Pratt
Chair
By Verner Panton
Gold bowl
Made from cigarette papers
Available from Heartworks

p.163
Beaded horse
From Monkeybiz Bead Project
Drawing
By William Kentridge

p.164-165
Ceramic pots
By Barbara Jackson
Artworks
By William Kentridge, Marlene Dumas
and Deborah Bell

Multimedia art
By Willie Bester
Plates
By Hylton Nel
Brown leather couch
By Matthew Hilton

p.166
Mirror
By Martine Jackson
Pots
By Barbara and Martine Jackson
Beaded doll
Available from Monkeybiz Bead Project

p.167
Blue shelf
From Lütge, Cape Town
Bright sculpture
By Norman Catherine
Beaded buck
Available from Monkeybiz Bead Project
Knopkieries (Zulu dancing sticks)
Can be sourced from Kim Sacks Gallery

p.169
Cement baboon
By Bulelani Nooi
Bird sculpture
Can be sourced from Totem Gallery

p.170-171
Barbershop signs
By the Nana Kwame Art Studio, Ghana
Crocodile and zebra lights:
By Michael Methven
Day bed
Can be sourced from Amatuli Fine Art,
Totem Gallery and Art Now
Body masks
Can be sourced from Amatuli Fine Art, Totem
Gallery and Art Now

p.172
Bead and wire lamp
Hand-beaded by Michael Methven

p.174-175
Animal-trophy light
By Michael Methven
Bead lamp
By Moonlight & Magic
Table
Can be sourced from Totem Gallery
Cloth
Can be sourced from Kim Sacks Gallery

p.176-177
Lights
By Michael Methven

p.179
Interiors
Astrid van der Heim
Mat
Available from Bright House and Philani
Weaving Project

p.180-181
Zulu sleeping mat holder
Available from Amatuli Fine Art

p.182-183
Photograph
David Ross for *Visi* magazine

p.184-85
Zulu sleeping mat holder
Available from Amatuli Fine Art

# DIRECTORY

Amatuli Fine Art
Tel: 011 440 5065

Andrew Makin – Architect
Tel: 031 303 5191
Email: designworkshop.kznia@saia.org.za

Anthony Harris and Gerhard Swart – Artists
Ceramic Matters
Tel: 011 701 3581
Email: ceramicm@mweb.co.za

Art Africa
Tel: 011 486 3193
Email: artafrica@yebo.co.za

Astrid van der Heim – Interior designer and dealer
Baroness von den Mess
Tel: 011 447 3371

Barbara Jackson – Potter
Mobile: 082 553 1015
Email: siren@iafrica.com
Website: www.barbarajackson.co.za

Boyd Ferguson
Tel: 021 425 5110

Bright House
Tel: 011 726 5657
Email: brighthouse@yebo.co.za

Clive van den Berg – Artist
Tel: 011 482 4089
Email: clivevdb@iafrica.com

Conservation Corporation Africa (Conscor)
Website: www.ccafrica.com

Deborah Bell – Artist
Email: Debuoybell@aol.com
Website: www.deborahbell.org

Design Team
Technikon Pretoria
Tel: 012 318 6002
Email: lisebutler@lantic.net

Dook – Photographer
Tel: 011 726 3568
Website: www.dookphoto.com

Durban Design Emporium
Tel: 031 201 2783

Egg Design
Tel: 031 313 8200
Website: www.eggandmilk.co.za

Estelle Lamprecht – Photographer
Mobile: 083 303 8370
Email: stella@new.co.za

European Concepts
Tel: 021 425 6565
Website: www.europeanconcepts.co.za

Felix Chikanya – Craftsman
Tel: 021 447 0213

Generation Furniture
Tel: 011 325 6302
Email: genfurn@mweb.co.za

Hans van der Merwe & Sons
Tel: 013 751 1540
Website: www.hansvandermerwe.co.za

Heartworks
Tel: 021 424 8419

Heidrun Diekman – Décor adviser
Tel: 09264 81 124 3225

Hylton Nel – Artist
Tel: 044 213 3899
Contact Peter Visser Gallery
Tel: 021 423 7870 or
Michael Stevenson Contemporary
Tel: 021 421 2575

ID Solutions
Tel: 021 422 3800
Website: www.idsolutions.co.za

Incanda: Décor Out of Africa
Tel: 021 872 2389
Head office: 011 781 0995

Jack's Camp
Uncharted Africa Safari Company
Tel: 267 241 2277 / 247 3575
Reservations:
Tel: 011 884 1346
Email: unchart.res@info.bw
Website: www.unchartedafrica.com

Jacqui Sinclair – Photographer
Contact The Photographers Gallery ZA
Tel: 021 422 2762

Joy Brasler – Architect
Tel: 031 303 1005
Email: joy@cecileandboyd.co.za

Julia Leakey – Product designer
Mobile (SA): 082 418 3662
Mobile (UK): 44 (0)788 789 1838
Email: julia_leakey@hotmail.com

Keanu Visser – Artist
Contact Peter Visser Gifts
Tel: 021 422 2660

Kim Sacks Gallery
Tel: 011 447 5804
Email: kim@kimsacksgallery.com

Leon Vermeulen – Artist
Tel: 044 382 1629

Lien Botha – Photographer
Mobile: 082 926 9005
Email: lienb@yebo.co.za

Lientjie Wessels – Artist, stylist and product developer
Contact Twig
Tel: 012 362 3188
Mobile: 082 531 6141

Limeline
Tel: 021 423 3540
Email: limeline@mweb.co.za
Website: www.limeline.co.za

Loads of Living
Head office
Tel: 011 700 3740
Website: www.loadsoflinen.co.za

LOSA (London-South Africa) Project
Tel: 011 883 7407

Louis Louw Johan Bergenthuin Architects
Tel: 011 781 3663
Fax: 011 781 3661

Lütge Gallery
Tel: 021 424 8448

Marlene Dumas – Artist
Website: www.postmedia.net/dumas/htt.htm

Martine Jackson – Artist
Tel: 021 424 8263
Mobile: 082 372 8062
Email: mjvisual@mweb.co.za

Merwelene van der Merwe – Photographer
Tel: 011 886 7886
Email: merwelene@icon.co.za

MG Design Box
Tel: 012 460 1965
Email: mgdesignbox@mweb.co.za

Monkeybiz Bead Project
Tel: 021 426 0145
Email: monkeybiz@iafrica.com
Website: www.monkeybiz.co.za

Montebello Design Centre
Tel: 021 686 8494

Moonlight and Magic
Tel: 021 843 3924
Email: moonlightandmagic@mweb.co.za

Mowani Mountain Camp
Website: www.mowani.com

Natalie Knight – The Art Source
Tel: 011 485 3606
Email: nknight@icon.co.za
Website: www.knightgall.com

Norman Catherine – Artist
Website: www.normancatherine.co.za

O + R Exclusive Creations
Tel: 011 463 6217

OKHA Interiors
Tel: 021 424 9706
Email: antoni@alternet.co.za
Website: www.okha.co.za

Pan African Market
Tel: 021 426 4478
Email: panafricanmarket@hotmail.com
Website: home.mweb.co.za/pa/pan

Philani Weaving Project
Tel: 021 387 5124

Philosophy
Tel: 021 462 6904

Plush Bazaar
Tel: 021 419 8328

Randall Moore Elephant Back Safaris
Website: www.elephantbacksafaris.com

Sarah Pratt – Artist
Tel: 021 448 1979

Silvio Rech and Lesley Carstens – Architects and interior designers
Mobile: 082 900 9935
Email: silviorech@hotmail.com

Singita Private Game Reserve
Tel: 021 683 3424
Website: www.singita.co.za

Stephen Inggs – Artist and photographer
Contact João Ferreira Gallery
Tel: 021 423 5403

Strauss Interiors
Tel: 021 554 2283

Fax: 021 554 2269
Email: davidstrauss@mweb.co.za

Streetwires
Tel: 021 426 2475
Email: info@streetwires.co.za
Website: www.streetwires.co.za

Tanya Komen – Interior designer
Email: tanjakomen@zol.co.zw

The Photographers Gallery ZA
Tel: 021 422 2762

The Scan Shop
Tel: 021 461 8382

Titus Steyn – Ceramicist
Contact OKHA Interiors
Tel: 021 424 9706 or
Peter Visser Gallery
Tel: 021 423 7870

Totem Gallery
Tel: 011 873 1266
Website: www.totemgallery.co.za
Branches:
The Firs Shopping Centre, Rosebank: 011 447 1409
Sandton City, Sandton: 011 884 6300

Willie Bester – Artist
Contact Association for Visual Arts
Tel: 021 424 7436
Website: www.goodman-gallery.com

William Kentridge – Artist
Website: www.goodman-gallery.com

Winston Rangwani – Artist and craftsman
Contact Streetwires
Tel: 021 426 2475

## References

Blauer, Ettagale. 1999. *African Elegance*, New Holland Publishers (UK), London.
Bromwell, Martyn (Ed). 1982. *The International Book of Wood*, AH, Artists House, London.
Chapman, Michael (Ed). 1981. *A Century of South African Poetry*, AD Donker, Craighall.
Dook. 1995. *Skin and Bone*, Dook Photography, Johannesburg.
Fiell, Charlotte & Peter. 1997. *1000 chairs*, Taschen, Köln
Foley, Tricia. 1993. *The Romance of Colonial Style*, Thames and Hudson, Ltd, London.
Fraser, Craig. 2002. *Shack Chic: Art and Innovation in South African Shack-lands*, Quivertree Publications, Cape Town.
Frescura, Franco. 1991. *Collected Essays on Southern African Architecture, 1980 – 1990*, University of Port Elizabeth, Port Elizabeth.
Goldblatt, David. 1998. *South Africa: The Structure of Things Then*, Oxford University Press, Cape Town.
Hall, Dinah. 1992. *Ethnic by Design*, Mitchell Beazley, London.
Pearse, G.E. 1956. *The Cape of Good Hope 1652 – 1833: An account of its buildings and the life of its people*, JL van Schaik, Ltd, Pretoria.
Pearse, G.E. 1968. *Eighteenth Century Architecture in South Africa*, AA Balkema, Cape Town.
Schofield, Jane. 1996. *Lime in Building: A Practical Guide*, Revised Second Edition, Cullompton Press, London.
Tambini, Michael. 1998. *The Look of the Century*, Dorling Kindersley Ltd, London.
Van Wyk, Johan, Conradie, Pieter and Constandaras, Nik (eds). 1988. *SA in Pöesie / SA in Poetry*, Owen Burgess Publishers, Pinetown.
Walton, James. 1956. *African Village*, JL Van Schaik, Pretoria.

# A special thanks to the following people for opening their doors to our photographers or helping with the production of *South*

- Ariane Besson
- Carrol Boyes and Barbara Jackson
- Conservation Corporation Africa (Conscor)
- David Strauss of Strauss Interiors
- Estelle Lamprecht
- Jenni Button of Philosophy
- Jack's Camp
- Michael and Anthea Methven
- Mowani Mountain Camp
- Randall Moore Elephant Back Safaris at Abu's Camp
- Silvio Rech and Lesley Carstens
- Singita Lebombo, Singita Boulders, Singita Ebony
- The Scan Shop
- Annelize Visser and Anton Sassenberg
- *Visi* magazine
- Anton Ressel of Streetwires
- Chris Zimberle of Limeline
- Sean Weldon of ID Solutions
- Yasmin Brand

First published in 2003 by
Tent Books (Pty) Ltd
waterhof@mweb.co.za

text: Les Aupiais

editorial co-ordinator: Janice Winter

sub editors:
Paul Wise
Barbara Mowatt

design: Massimo Cecconi

cover design: Anton Sassenberg

production manager: Toni Venturini

photographer: Massimo Cecconi

contributing photographers:
Alain Proust: p.130, p.132
Craig Fraser, from *Shack Chic*: p.156
David Ross, for *Visi* magazine: p.182-183
Dook: p.48-51, p.121-127
Paul Gordon: p.140

assistant to authors: Doeda Mathidza

Reproduction by Hirt and Carter Cape (Pty) Ltd
Printed and bound by Tien Wah Press, Singapore

Distributed by Quivertree Publications cc
PO Box 51051
Waterfront
8002
Cape Town
South Africa
Tel: +27 (0)21 461 6808
Fax: +27 (0)21 461 6842
Email: info@quivertree.co.za
Website: www.quivertree.co.za

ISBN 0-620-30890-7